obit.

obit.

Inspiring stories of ordinary people
who led extraordinary lives

Jim Sheeler

PRUETT PUBLISHING COMPANY
BOULDER, COLORADO

The stories collected in this work were previously published in the *Rocky Mountain News, Denver Post* and *Boulder Planet*.

First Printing 2007

Library of Congress Cataloging-in-Publication Data

Sheeler, Jim.
  Obit. : Inspiring stories of ordinary people who led extraordinary lives / Jim Sheeler. — 1st ed.
    p. cm.
  ISBN 978-0-87108-943-4 (alk. paper)
  1. Colorado—Biography. 2. Biography—20th century.
  3. Obituaries—Colorado. I. Title.
  CT226.S54 2007
  978.8'033092--dc22
  [B]

                                        2006039006

Introduction

"THESE PEOPLE NEED CANCER," she said.

Aimee Grunberger didn't mean it to sound vindictive. As usual, she was just being brutally honest.

A few weeks before the forty-four-year-old died of breast cancer, she had sat on her porch, trying to read the newspaper. Instead she found herself consumed by all the petty squabbles and useless bickering she had recently noticed more than ever.

"These people need cancer," she had told her husband. "Not enough to kill them, just enough to make them see what's important."

Inside their home a few weeks later, her husband looked at what was left of the candle that was supposed to last for seven days of mourning. Like his wife, it burned out too early.

He stared at the candle. Then he looked at me.

"It's not that there's too much cancer in the world," he said. "It's just that it's badly distributed."

Most of the people in this book will die before the fifth paragraph. You probably haven't heard of any of them. That doesn't mean it's a book about nobodies. That doesn't mean it's a book about death.

This is a book—as Aimee Grunberger might have said—about what is important.

As an obituary writer, the most frequent question I'm asked is how I deal with it; how sad it must be to write these stories. The thing is, it's just the opposite.

The death beat is supposed to be the worst job in the newsroom. For those of us who understand, it's journalism's best kept secret—a place of raw emotion and endless wisdom, a place where you find lessons of life more brilliant than anything you'll ever find from the traditionally designated "noteworthy" people who usually appear in the rest of the newspaper.

It's a place where you learn that someone like Aimee Grunberger can't be defined in a single word such as "author," "homemaker," "poet," "mother," or "teacher." And she is far from alone.

When Johnny Richardson died, he was buried in a pauper's grave; his entire estate fit inside a cardboard container the size of a shoebox. When first printed in the newspaper, he had the shortest obituary on the page:

Jonathan "Johnny" Richardson of Denver, a shoe-shine worker, died August 13 in Denver. He was 74. No services were held. He was born June 24, 1925. His interest was listening to jazz. There are no immediate survivors.

Richardson's life story is one of the longest I've written.

While mining the jazz bars and barber shops, looking for information on Richardson, I constantly thought about the man looking up from his shoeshine box at the airport, listening to other peoples' stories, rarely sharing his own.

Maybe the stories of life in this collection will coax a few more people to ask about those stories. Maybe it will even encourage more people to interview their own friends, parents, plumbers, and possibly even the guy who shines their shoes.

"You know, he always was going to write a book about his life," Richardson's old girlfriend told me, "about all the stories of his life."

In many ways, this book also belongs to him.

WHEN I BEGAN WRITING OBITUARIES, my goal was to write about people whose names had never appeared in the newspaper, to find the stories that had never been told—and, just as important, the lessons they left behind.

When interviewing friends and relatives, one of the questions I always ask is, "What did you learn from this person's life?"

It's a question that rarely elicits a quick response—which is understandable. Try to answer it yourself: what did you learn from your (wife, husband, mother, father, sister, best friend ...). The answers are always different, and they're rarely concise.

Some of those answers are revealed in the obituaries I've included in this book; many more are only hinted at, deep inside the story.

For me, the answer is simple: these people teach me how to live.

For Miss Betty, the POG

Contents

How to Build a Mountain

Edward C. 'Duke' Mallory

EVERY DAY, THE BOY COULD BE FOUND at the same place on that big Missouri farm. For hours he would shovel dirt into a bucket and carry it over to a certain spot, where he would dump it onto a pile.

As the sun set, the boy would climb the dirt and look out at the prairie. Each day he stood a little bit higher.

As the years passed, some of the kids made fun of him. Adults just shook their heads. The boy continued to dig.

When they asked him why, the boy tried to explain what he had seen during his family's brief trip to Colorado when he was three years old. He had seen something he couldn't forget.

Edward Mallory was building a mountain.

As she sat back in her wheelchair at her home in Wheat Ridge, Frances Mallory smiled as she retold her husband's story.

"He worked for several years on that mountain of his," she said. "He'd dig the dirt and cart it up there. He said he had no doubt that he would build his own mountain. And he got it up pretty high.

"I don't think I've ever known anyone as drawn to the mountains as my husband," she said. "Lots of people like the mountains. But the mountains were his kindred spirits."

Edward Mallory would eventually spend much of his lifetime scouring backcountry trails throughout the state he once dreamed of. He rarely told anyone what he was looking for but always described in detail what he found.

More than eight decades later, hundreds of people scurry up the dirt and rocks every year, looking for the place that bears his name.

As a boy, he built a mountain. As a man, he went inside.

Edward Carson Mallory died on December 17, 1998. He was eighty-five.

When Edward Mallory was ten years old, his family moved to Colorado, and the boy—nicknamed "Duke" by his father—quickly forgot his fake mountain for the real Rockies. Within a few years, he had already mapped in his mind the trails around Boulder, hiking thousands of miles up and across the Continental Divide.

That's when he began the story of The Cave.

I was beginning to feel restless, he wrote in his journal. *I wanted to find some new adventures, lonely places to explore and things that others did not know about.*

I was now almost 18 years old.

On a cold winter night, Mart Parsons, the ranger, and I were talking about the mountains as we often did.

"Mart," I said. "I want to hike in country where no one ever goes. I like to explore."

The ranger had heard stories about a hole deep in the hills west of Boulder but wasn't sure if the stories were true. Miners had supposedly stumbled upon a large cave during the 1800s, where they had cut down some nearby trees.

"No one ever goes into that place," the ranger told the boy. "There aren't even any trails."

Mallory began to climb.

INSIDE THE WHEAT RIDGE HOME they shared for twenty-six of their fifty-six years together, Frances Mallory scanned bookshelves filled with nature books and photos of her husband's travels.

"He saw things you didn't see," she said. "He identified every tree, and then he would go back and look it up and index it and categorize it. He studied it, and it was important to him, not because he was going to do anything special with the study, but because it was there. It was important because it was part of life and it was there."

She pointed to a display case, one designed to show off fine crystal or china. The case sparkled with chunks of mountains.

"That's amethyst," she said, pointing to the rocks. "That's amber."

The rocks are souvenirs of the places he walked in his spare time and the passion that became his career as a chemist with the

U.S. Geological Survey in Denver, where he worked for more than thirty years.

"He felt they were doing work that wouldn't be done otherwise," his wife said. "It was just to find pure knowledge."

AFTER SPENDING THE ENTIRE SUMMER of 1932 searching for the cave the ranger had described, Mallory found himself high in the hills, staring at an opening "black as midnight."

I moved slowly towards the opening, he wrote. *Standing just inside, I waited for my eyes to adjust to the darkness. When I saw that I was standing in a large room, I began feeling my way toward the back. Gliding out of the darkness came something with a four-foot wingspan, its claws extended and ready to attack. I ducked the moment before a hawk sailed over my head.*

After exploring the cave, he returned to Boulder and took the ranger back to the cave. The ranger would later try to find it himself but would fail. For the rest of the summer, the cave's sole visitors were Mallory and his dog.

We had the cave all to ourselves, and spent many happy, relaxed hours there, watching the world laid out below us like a giant map, he wrote. *I enjoyed listening to the winds blowing through the trees and around the many tall rocky spires. Hawks would glide silently over the nearby pinnacles and spires to the east. In the afternoon great thunderheads, stormy blue and shining white, sometimes reaching a height of seventy thousand feet, would form above the prairie near the eastern horizon.*

At the ranger's instruction, the young man returned to the cave and painted his name nearby. Noticing the tree stumps made by the miners, he refused to say he was the first to find the spot. Instead, underneath his name he painted a single word—a word with more than one meaning for the boy who once dreamed of Colorado:

"Rediscovered."

ON THE FLOOR OF THE MALLORY HOME, boxes filled with thousands of pages of typed notes tell the story of his life through his hikes.

"Can you imagine anyone doing all this—not for money, not for fame, but just for pure pleasure?" Frances Mallory asked, holding up the pages. "Just for pure pleasure."

Among all the pages, there was one story he did not write.

"Five years ago he went over on that new road to Glenwood Springs," she began. "That night he went out to hike."

It was just after his eightieth birthday. Just before he would be diagnosed with cancer.

"He went out to hike," she continued. "And where he went I don't know."

Duke Mallory rarely told anyone what he was looking for. As the sun went down that night, he walked up the dirt for the last time.

"He was saying goodbye to them," Frances Mallory said quietly.

"He was saying goodbye to the mountains."

Life's Lessons
Learned Too Soon

Daniel Seltzer

AT THE TOP OF THE PAGE, the title is scrawled in the impulsive script of a fourteen-year-old boy: "Code of Morals." Near the bottom of the page is a signature, "Daniel Seltzer 5-24-98."

Between them, words to live by and to leave behind.

1. All moral decisions should be weighed by determining if the overall benefits outweigh the costs.

"I found the list in his drawer, while I was going through his room," said Fern Seltzer, as she looked over the words scribbled on notebook paper in her son Daniel's handwriting.

"Occasionally he would refer to these," she said. "He would recite them from memory. He put a lot of effort into them."

2. Religion only brings about hatred, war, and conflict; never peace or unity.

His Code of Morals includes the words of great thinkers and some of his own, adopted and narrowed down to ten guidelines. The list was not completed for a class. Nobody told him to write it. As with most of Daniel Seltzer's passions, it was sparked by a searing quest for knowledge—a search that would pile a lifetime of learning into a body that was never old enough to drive a car.

Daniel Seltzer died suddenly and unexpectedly at home February 13, 1999, of complications from a previously undetected heart condition. He was fifteen.

3. Never allow fear to run one's life.

Born in Oregon, Daniel Seltzer moved with his family to Denver when he was an infant. He crawled at six months, walked at ten months, and could identify the alphabet before he was two. He began reading to himself shortly afterward. His favorite book in kindergarten was Judy Blume's *Tales of a Fourth Grade Nothing.*

"He was," his mother said, "in a hurry."

4. Inanimate objects are never inherently good or evil.

On Daniel Seltzer's bookshelf are his mother's copies of plays by Euripides and Dante's *Paradiso,* along with his own fantasy books and science fiction collections from Isaac Asimov. Nearby rests an autographed copy of a program from a Central City Opera production of *The Barber of Seville.* In front of his room are certificates from the Odyssey of the Mind competition.

Above the bed in his room hang two plaques from the University of Denver's Rocky Mountain Talent Search, recognizing Daniel's score of 1500 on the Scholastic Aptitude Test (out of a possible 1600)—at the age of thirteen.

On his bed is a well-worn, tattered, teddy bear.

"A beautiful adult mind," one of his school counselors wrote about Daniel, "in the body of a magical little boy."

5. Know one's own limitations.

Jean Strop remembers walking into Cherry Creek High School with Daniel when he was a student at Cherry Hills Village Elementary School, and she was his teacher in the gifted and talented student program. Daniel wanted to build a laser.

"He was one of those kids who from early on I expected to do great things, that he would solve some problem that would change the world, someone who would make some contribution," Strop said. "He was pretty intense at learning, mastering, doing well. He had big plans."

"I think he was a great observer of life," she said after reading his Code of Morals. "He was a special soul."

6. Simple things have simple answers; complex things have complex answers.

Daniel Seltzer's music collection spanned the centuries, but rarely made it to the twentieth. His appreciation for opera and live theater continued to widen until a week before his death, when he attended a Denver Center Theater Company production of *The Rivals* with his father. Afterward, he devoured the script.

"Two years ago he saw (the opera) *Don Giovanni*. ...We had to go to the library and check out both versions of *Don Giovanni* on videotape, we had to go buy the CD, we had to have the cassette tapes," Fern Seltzer said. "We listened to *Don Giovanni* ten hours a day. He sat there with the libretto and followed along in Italian. I'm sorry to say he could not sing. We were sitting there one time on the couch watching *The Marriage of Figaro* and he was sitting next to me croaking along. It was so horrible sounding, but it was also so cute. He knew that libretto, too. Instead of doing his homework, he sat up learning the libretto."

In school, his classes were advanced. Still, his parents say, he often struggled to balance schoolwork with his true passions.

"It didn't interest him to have all A's. He just felt that he wanted to learn, and it didn't matter if it was something that was directly applicable to school," his mother said.

"I do wonder if, somehow, he knew that his time was limited."

7. Only perform desperate measures when in desperate situations.

As she stood near the corner of her son's bed, Fern Seltzer remembered the last morning of Daniel's life. He had been home with a mild case of the flu; as she sat at his bedside, there was no way to know that his heart was failing.

"He had a structural heart defect. If he hadn't have gotten the flu, he presumably wouldn't have died now, but would have later. The coroner told me there were only forty cases of this in the medical literature. ... If we had known about it, the only thing that would have saved him would have been a heart transplant but there was no way to know that he needed one."

She paused.

"It's hard to come to terms with that."

8. Never allow anger to cloud one's own judgment.

When he was eight months old, Daniel was underneath the sink, unscrewing pipes. At a year old, he was taking apart cameras. He turned off the escalators at department stores and pulled the fire alarm at school. Once, he ran off inside an airport and almost boarded a plane to Newark.

Diagnosed with attention deficit hyperactivity disorder, the adult mind in the little boy's body could often make for more than a handful.

"He was just very determined," his mother said, "and of course that made him difficult."

It also, however, made for stirring moments of joy, his parents say, such as the time when Daniel, as a very young boy, first saw the U.S. Capitol.

"It wasn't just child's excitement; it was a different kind of excitement," said his father, Roger Seltzer. "He appreciated where he was. He appreciated what it meant."

9. People are, despite all their faults, inherently "good."

Daniel's computer was an older model, long past obsolescence. Instead of buying a new one, the boy preferred the challenge of continually upgrading the machine by himself. He had, after all, been playing with computers since he was two years old.

"He'd have his thumb in his mouth and would bob up and down typing words," said his father. "That's a very vivid memory. Part of that was just the sheer determination. He just loved the computer, even at that age."

For years, he helped people with computer problems and had began a business capitalizing on his talent.

"Early on, he didn't take a fee," his mother said. "Just milk and cookies."

During the few years before his death, he built friendships on the Internet, particularly with groups of people involved in fantasy role-playing games. In tribute to him, friends devoted a web site to him.

"He always commented on my ideas and stories when everyone else could care less," wrote a friend that Daniel never met in person. *"He was always nice to me, and for that I thank him. As a memento, I'm going to leave him on my contact list as long as I can. ... The only thing that can delete him is if my computer crashes."*

10. Remember, but do not worship, the past; live for, but not only for, the present, and prepare for, but do not panic over, the future.

Number 10 was initially the last of Daniel's codes, followed by his signature, and the date, 5-24-98.

Two weeks before his fifteenth birthday, he decided to add one more.

11. Nothing is of more importance than love.

The Marine Who
Wasn't Afraid to Cry

William B. Chapple Jr.

THE THREE OLD FRIENDS SAT AT THE TABLE telling war stories, remembering the one about the Marine who wasn't afraid to cry.

"At Tarawa, 5,500 went ashore," said Russell Ratcliff. "There were 3,166 casualties."

Ratcliff wore a satin blue jacket emblazoned "Second Marine Division," the first group ashore at Tarawa Island, one of the bloodiest battles in the Pacific.

"There were guys shot while getting out of the damn amphibious tractor. They were getting shot all around us. Some drowned. There were bodies in the sea floating like corks in a bathtub. ... When we got ashore, the fighting was eyeball to eyeball."

Somewhere in the chaos of the first wave of Tarawa, 1943— and, before that, the legendary battle at Guadalcanal—was Private First Class William B. Chapple. Every man involved in those battles has stories. "Chappie" never shared them.

"At a (Marine Corps) birthday party a few years ago, all the guys got together to tell about the times they remembered during the war," said Jack Hare, president of the Colorado chapter of the Second Marine Division Association.

"When they got to Chappie, he started crying," Hare said. "He couldn't talk about it."

"He just kept it inside of himself," Ratcliff said.

"That's OK," Hare said.

Among a collection of photos, the veterans found a picture of young Chappie as a farm boy, and a group photo of the twenty-year-old's military enlistment class.

"You never forget the names," Ratcliff said, while looking at the photo of the young Marines. "The reason they add an extra week onto boot camp? It's to teach you what the hell a friend is."

William Bryan "Chappie" Chapple Jr. died January 10, 2000. He was seventy-eight.

THE BOUND POCKET-SIZED BOOK is titled, "My Life in the Service. The diary of William B. Chapple, Jr."

"In the beginning of the journal, he's all gung-ho," said Debbie DiFiore, one of Chapple's daughters. "But near the middle he says, 'Maybe I'm not cut out for this.'"

"He wrote in that book constantly, and then there's one entry that a friend of his committed suicide," said Ed Chapple, one of his sons. "After that, he never wrote in the journal again."

Near the book is a photo album and letters the young private sent to his mother. There are pictures of Chappie with the Jeep he nicknamed "Jean," long before he knew he would marry a woman with the same name. There are pictures of tanks and guns. There are pictures of skeletons and corpses.

Chapple returned from the Pacific in 1944, stricken with malaria, and spent a year in a military hospital before being honorably discharged. When he returned to his family's tiny Kansas farm, he began where he left off, as a mechanic. He met Jean Ward at the Ford dealership, married her soon afterwards, and the couple began a family.

In the late 1950s, Chapple heard there was good work in a little Colorado town called Aurora. The family moved from Kansas to Colorado on Armistice Day, 1959.

Chapple never talked to his wife about the war. He never told his kids more than bits and pieces of stories, never talked about the disease that kept him in the hospital for so long. Still, everyone in the family always knew he was a Marine.

"He'd wake us up the same way every morning, by saying 'Get up and pee, the world's on fire!'" Ed Chapple said, smiling.

"Late at night when the national anthem would come on to sign off the television station, we would all stand," remembered daughter Patricia "Casey" Chapple. "He'd say, 'I don't care how late it is. You stand up.' We stood."

Occasionally, the kids would watch war movies with their father and see him cry. Sometimes he had to turn off the movie before it was over. Sometimes they would hear him in the bathroom, sobbing.

The tears, however, were not always of loss.

"A while back we were at Old Chicago restaurant in Aurora and there was a bunch of Marines sitting at a table," DiFiore said. "One of the guys saw his (Second Division) cap and came up and said 'Sir, it's a privilege to shake your hand.'

"He cried after that, too."

INSIDE THE CHAPPLE HOME in Aurora, nobody ever asks for the time.

At the top of the hour, dozens of clocks chirp and whistle. They ring at every quarter-hour. They were only one of Chappie's noisy collections.

"On Guadalcanal and Tarawa the noise was dependable. You had to worry when it was quiet. He didn't like the quiet," said Patricia Chapple. "At home, the clocks were always going off. The radio was always playing quietly."

Chappie's favorite background noise was that of the car. Any car. In his spare time he would buy junkers and fix them up for resale—if he wasn't already helping a family member with a car of his or her own.

"You would call him on the phone and hold the receiver to the car and he could tell you what was wrong," DiFiore said.

Chappie worked as a mechanic at Deane Buick for a decade, where his reputation for practical jokes spread quickly.

"He was such a joker. He would bolt guys' lunchboxes to the table," Ed Chapple said. "When a mechanic went under the hood, he would honk the horn."

As the clocks chime inside the Chapple home, tears still blend into laughter.

"We're a very emotional family. That was part of him, the humor and the sadness," DiFiore said. "Sunny side of the street. He was always looking for that." But sometimes the memories were too strong.

In the 1970s, Chapple's increasing disability caused by the effects of malaria forced him into early retirement, so he took care of the kids while Jean went to work at Woolco for the next twenty years. The grown children still giggle while remembering the practical jokes he would play while watching them.

"Dad is a dichotomy," Patricia Chapple said. "He is this tragic, flawed hero who's seen such horror, and at the other end of the spectrum he was such a clown."

Along with the clocks, Chapple also collected cameras—mostly cheap, thrift-store, sometimes-broken cameras, many of which he would try to fix, using up old rolls of film taking pictures of the family.

"The clocks represent the time we've spent together," Patricia said. "And he collected the cameras to capture it."

DURING THE PAST FEW YEARS, the remaining men of the Second Marine Division have seen plenty of burial ceremonies. They know the meanings of each triangular fold of the flag. They've heard the words, "On behalf of a grateful nation," and the mournful "Taps."

The Marine Corps color guard was waiting for the hearse when it arrived at Fort Logan on January 14. William Chapple was buried with his uniform, one of about 1,100 World War II veterans who die every day.

A few days earlier, he had been rushed to the hospital, concerned about an aneurysm that had bothered him for the past two years.

"At the hospital, they said that with the aneurysm there was a 100 percent chance he would die, with surgery there was 75 to 95 percent chance he'd die on the table. He didn't crack a tear," Ed Chapple said. "He said, 'Let's try it.' And he never shed a tear when I said goodbye to him, when I kissed him and said 'I love you.'

"That's the last thing he said to all of us."

At the first shots of the twenty-one-gun salute, many of the mourners flinched at the noise. The military veterans stood steady.

The flag was taken from the coffin and folded into a triangle. When the Marine handed it to Jean Chapple, his voice cracked.

"On behalf of a grateful nation," the young Marine said.

The family remains in awe at what happened next.

"I was looking at the Marine who didn't even know my dad," DiFiore said.

"There were tears coming down his cheeks."

The Magician Who Saved His Best Trick for Last

Robert E. Schmidt

THE ADVERTISEMENTS SHOUT with vaudevillian verve from yellowed newspapers and posters, in words that still sound like Bob Schmidt.

"LADIES AND GENTLEMEN, BOYS AND GIRLS," they blare,

"SEE the 20th CENTURY ALADDIN. A MAN OF MAGIC AND MYSTERY."

In the sepia-tone promotional photos, a dapper man in a tuxedo stands beside a levitating woman. In another photo he lies in a box, chained impossibly tight.

"CAN he ESCAPE? See THIS and MANY OTHER TRICKS."

Inside Schmidt's Denver home, nearly nine decades of magic pours through the living room. The guillotine. The escape-proof box. The black top hat that birthed thousands of rabbits. The wand that so many ladies and gentlemen, boys and girls, truly believed held a special sort of magic.

As the Schmidt family search through the boxes of tricks and scrapbooks inside the old magician's house, they remember the acts they marveled at, then find a relic from the 1930s they had never seen before: a sign the size of a card table—the biggest advertisement of them all.

"My brother and I found it and we had the same idea," says his son, Kim Schmidt. "At first we thought, 'Is this appropriate?' Then we agreed, Dad would love it."

At Bob Schmidt's funeral, his family placed the billboard where they knew it belonged: right next to the coffin.

"CHAINED, SHACKLED AND HANDCUFFED," the sign read, "LOCKED IN A MAILBAG AND SECURELY NAILED AND ROPED INTO THIS BOX . . . PROFESSOR SCHMIDT EMERGES —INSTANTANEOUSLY AND FREE OF ALL HIS BONDS!"

Robert E. Schmidt, aka "Magician Bob Damon," aka "Professor Schmidt," aka "The 20th Century Aladdin," died May 9, 2002, of a blood infection. He was ninety.

INSIDE THE TRAVELING CARNIVALS in the early 1900s a certain youngster was known to pop his head into the tents, coaxing the performers to share a few secrets. During the day, little Bobby helped his parents sell portrait photographs at exhibitions throughout the country; it wasn't long before the boy had become "Professor Schmidt," constantly honing his dexterous hands along with his stage shtick.

In the 1930s he earned a drama degree from Northern State Teacher's College in South Dakota, then joined the Civilian Conservation Corps, working on construction projects across the country and entertaining the exhausted men at the end of the day. At the onset of World War II, his booming voice and ambitious tricks earned him a place with the United Service Organizations.

Before the group left to tour overseas during the war, an agent suggested he not perform with a German surname, so Schmidt looked through his family tree and found an aunt named Damon; the stage name stuck.

While performing with the USO, he played shows literally all the way to Timbuktu—ninety-three countries and islands in all. It wasn't until the last one that he met the woman who would accompany him the rest of his life.

A Denver native who played organ with the all-female Joy Cayler band, Livvy Taylor was stationed in Japan, homesick, waiting for a letter from Colorado or a transfer back home when she first saw her future husband pull a rabbit out of his hat.

"When we met, I was more interested in M-A-I-L than M-A-L-E," she says, laughing as usual. The pair were soon together onstage and off. They married on his birthday—January 1, and she accompanied him on organ as the pair participated in variety shows throughout the country.

As television's popularity sucked the life from many of the live shows in the 1950s, the couple settled in Denver, where Schmidt took a job at Neusteters department store selling sportswear—a job he would hold on and off until the 1980s. Meanwhile, he couldn't give up the stage.

In the late 1950s the couple joined on as part of Pete Smythe's "East Tincup" Old West theme park near Golden, where Schmidt wowed crowds with his Houdini-like escapes and giant props, such as his hand-made guillotine, relying on his stage patter as much as the trick itself.

With the "head-chopper" trick, for instance, he would slice an apple in half with the machine, then lock a volunteer's head into place, telling him to hold onto his ears when the blade drops, so he could hoist the dismembered noggin up high once it was lopped off. Schmidt would then begin mumbling to himself, pretending to have no idea what he was doing, and just before the blade dropped, he would hold up the front page of a newspaper, ostensibly from the previous town he played.

"DAMON BEHEADS MAN," the headline screamed; inevitably, so did the volunteer.

In the late 1970s, Schmidt got a small taste of Hollywood, so to speak, landing a role in the low-budget film, *The Legend of Alfred Packer,* playing the role of Israel Swann—the first man supposedly devoured by the infamous cannibal.

"I remember turning on the television late one night and thinking, 'I know that guy—the one being eaten,' " remembers his son, Rick. " 'Hey, that's Dad!' "

After retiring from Neusteters, Schmidt returned to magic full time, traveling with a Chautauqua group and performing at hundreds of birthday parties for children, where he mesmerized the kids without talking down to them—allowing them to think they had the trick figured out, then blowing their minds.

"It's hard work, and it's a dedication thing. Plus, you really have to be a ham," says Rick Schmidt. "And Dad was a pure, dyed-in-the-wool ham. A true showman."

As THEY AGED, THE SCHMIDTS continued to perform for people who truly needed a good escape: developmentally disabled children, elderly people at nursing homes, patients in hospitals—along with dozens more.

"Your magic was the right medicine," wrote a nurse from Mercy Medical Center, after one of his many shows.

Even into his late eighties, Bob Schmidt continued to work at birthday parties and at the Renaissance Festival, where, as an aged, gray-bearded magician walking around the grounds performing sleight-of-hand tricks, people truly believed he was Merlin.

Though he never officially gave up magic, the number of shows diminished until he could barely stand. Still, there was one trick he never forgot.

"At the beginning of every show, he would take out an alarm clock and put a satin handkerchief over it, and he would say, 'I only have a certain amount of time to do this for you,' " remembers his son, Rick.

Throughout the whole show, the clock would sit onstage, ticking away. Few spectators would notice it until the last trick.

"At the end of the show, the clock would ring, and he would walk over to it and say, 'Boy, doesn't time disappear,'" Rick Schmidt says.

"He would take the handkerchief off, and the clock was gone."

Living in the Blink

Lois A. Engel

BOB ENGEL PARKS HIS CAR in a patch of overgrown weeds near the railroad tracks in eastern Colorado, at a place where the train no longer stops.

"This is it," he says. "This is where the depot was. This is where my mother was born."

He walks along in the weeds and dry wheat and pauses under an old cottonwood tree.

"My grandparents planted these trees," he says. "There's not much left, now."

In the back of his car sits a vase full of roses, cut from his backyard in Denver. Whenever he comes back to Agate, he always brings roses for his mother and his aunt. Today, his aunt will get them all.

He walks out of the weeds and shakes his head.

"The railroad really should take better care of this place," he says.

Agate, population seventy, is one of those towns that people describe as "blink and you'll miss it."

Lois A. Engel loved living in the blink.

FROM A STACK OF PHOTOS, Bob Engel pulls out a picture of his mother in a baby carriage, parked near the railroad tracks. Both her parents were Colorado natives, and her father was a telegrapher for the Union Pacific for fifty-four years. They figured it was only natural their kids would be born in the depot.

The family lived the 1920s in the railroad-built housing near the tracks, enduring the fierce windstorms, snow, and torrential dust that coated the area. Along with the dust came the Depression.

Among his mother's possessions, Bob Engel finds a letter written when his mother was nine years old, in 1931, after she had lost a tooth.

Dear fairies, the letter begins, *I don't suppose you will bring me anything because all the banks went busted, but bring me a dime if you can. Well, I will close with love, Lois D.*

It was a time that would shape the family for the rest of their lives. When Lois married railroad worker George Engel and had children, they lived in a railroad station manager's house and then in a twenty-by-ten-foot homesteaders' shack. The family didn't get electricity or running water until the 1950s.

"We were poor, but we didn't know it," Engel says. "She always said, 'Whatever you're dealt, you deal with it.'"

THE HOUSE THAT USED TO SIT near the depot now rests a mile and a half from the tracks. George Engel bought the building in the 1950s, when the railroad pulled out and the interstate came in—about the time they say the town began to fade.

As the kids grew up, Lois Engel worked as a cook at the Agate Café.

"She could make dinner rolls that were like cake," her son says. "Her meatloaf, her fried chicken ..." he trails off, tasting the words.

The café is now gone, like most everything in the town that was there during the first half of the century. The grocery store closed down, and the hotel burned years ago. Another fire last year claimed another three historic buildings on the main street.

"Our whole town has burned," Engel says. "It's left a hole in our hearts."

Lois Engel worked for the Agate public school as a secretary and as a bus driver, keeping track of the town's kids the way her parents once kept track of the town.

"She really cared for those kids," says her sister, Louise Mohler, who still lives in Agate. "She fought for those kids."

As farm prices fluctuated, she continued to take jobs, working as the area's last justice of the peace. Her sons say she was strict but fretted about each fine she handed down. She even married a few couples but was frustrated when the marriages didn't last.

When George Engel died in 1989, she had been married to him a few months shy of fifty years.

EVERY TIME BOB ENGEL nears the Agate exit on I-70, he sees what most people ignore. He notices the town's missing water tower, the one that now sits in the historic Pioneer Village in Nebraska. He misses the depot, which was later moved to Yoder, where it is used as a residence.

He can point to a dilapidated wooden shack in the middle of a wheat field, and recite its history.

"See that house?" Engel asks while driving down Interstate 70. "My grandma homesteaded there."

It's pioneer knowledge that was passed on by his mother, he says, and to her by her mother. That appreciation for history is apparent in a newspaper interview in the *Limon Leader* given in the late 1980s by Lois Engel's mother, Hilda Duenweg.

"There's a lot of history in these places—Agate, River Bend, Buick. It's too bad that it isn't well preserved," the ninety-three-year-old told the newspaper. "But who cares? No one cares anymore."

THESE DAYS, EIGHTEEN-WHEELERS have taken the place of steam locomotives, roaring past the old railroad house on the Engel farm. Lois Engel's family says the noise never really bothered her. She played what she was dealt.

During the CB radio craze of the 1970s and '80s, Lois Engel kept her ears tuned to truckers' conversations as they whizzed by on I-70. Her handle was "grandma." When travelers would run out of gas on the highway, she would invite them inside.

"She sure did have a sense of humor," Bob Engel says. "She would get to giggling and just wouldn't stop."

Five years ago a stroke forced Lois Engel from the home she lived in nearly all her life, and she moved to an assisted care facility twenty miles away, in Limon. Her kids asked her to stay with them, but they say she would have none of it. She died August 4, 1999, at the age of seventy-seven.

Before the stroke, Lois was known as the oldest Agate native still living in the town. These days the honor has been passed to her sister, Louise Mohler, who served thirty-three years as the town's postmaster.

BACK IN BOB ENGEL'S CAR, his aunt is in the passenger seat. The car kicks up a cloud of dust as they travel out of town, past the old Engel farm and into the winding bluffs that only a few farmers know about.

"Mom said the prettiest time of the morning was driving that school bus out here. The sun would come up over these hills," he says. "She would watch the sunrise and remember it. She would come home talking about the sun hitting the frost on the ground."

The two ride quietly for a few minutes as they pass fields of wheat and sunflowers, and Engel stops the car on a hill at the top of the valley.

"There's our little town," Mohler says.

"From out here, if you look at it right," he says, "it looks a lot bigger than it really is."

A Lifetime Together;
Death Four Days Apart

John and Carmella Scordo

THE BUNDLE OF CRINKLY, YELLOWING ENVELOPES is wrapped carefully in white silk and tied with a blue ribbon. The addresses all begin the same: To Carmella Perrino.

I haven't seen you for the longest time. ... If you have any boyfriends, drop 'em. If you're engaged to anyone, break it. Because I'm going to marry you.

George Scordo smiled as he slid his father's letter back into the envelope and pulled out another one.

"This one he sent to her September 26, 1932," Scordo said, opening the letter.

Dearest Sugar, I just got home and found your letter waiting for me.

Scordo's voice cracked and he swallowed, catching the emotions. He then began to paraphrase.

"He says, 'Send me your picture.' He tells her that he still wants to marry her. Ah, look at this, look how he signs it:

To my dream girl. A world of love. Millions of kisses for you and you alone. John Joseph Scordo.

Scordo tucked the letter back into the stack and slowly retied the blue ribbon.

"Usually with death, there is a lot of remorse, a lot of sadness," he said. "But this is a happy story. This is a neat story.

"This is an incredible love story."

Carmella M. Scordo died February 11, 1999. She was eighty-one. John J. Scordo died four days later. He was eighty-three.

THE AREA IN NORTHWEST DENVER that began as a haven for Italian immigrants to Colorado remains a place where neighbors know each other by more than a wave. It's an area where John and Carmella Scordo were known by their hugs.

"Walk down this street, mention John and Carmie, and you just see if anyone you talk to doesn't get a smile on their face," said Ed Westerkamp, who—along with his wife June—lived next door to the Scordos for the past forty-five years.

"If you were nice to them, they were twice as nice to you—they had to repay you twenty-five times for one favor," Westerkamp said. "Both of 'em were sweethearts."

The couple met in junior high at Mount Carmel School, the parochial center of the neighborhood, where they grew up three blocks from each other. They began dating then and never stopped.

"If there were more people like them," Westerkamp said, "there would be no reason to have a police department."

A few days after Carmella's death, Westerkamp was standing in the neighborhood grocery store when another neighbor caught him.

"She asked if I had heard what happened," Westerkamp said. "She said, 'Carmie came back and got John.'"

FROM THE DOZENS OF PHOTO ALBUMS compiled by his father, George Scordo pulled out one labeled "Scrapbook" and turned to the first page.

Our 'life' began the day we were married, 1937, June 6, his father had written in indelible red marker.

Inside the scrapbook, the couple kept dozens of wedding photos—even the receipt for her wedding dress ($39.27, including tax, from Daniels & Fisher).

Through the pages, the pictures reflect the big, stoic man and his wife's seemingly constant smile.

As the years progressed, John Scordo worked for a school supply company and Carmella volunteered endless hours at Our Lady of Mount Carmel Church while also working in the bridal department at Neusteters department store.

"She was exceedingly generous," said Rosa Mazone, one of the Scordos' nieces. "She would give somewhere between fifty and seventy-five gifts every Christmas, and she remembered every birthday."

They continued the tradition of inviting family members and friends over for elaborate Italian feasts, sharing kitchen duties.

"He always said his sauce was better," said George Scordo, pointing to a photo showing the couple in front of a massive plate of spaghetti and meatballs.

Scordo continued turning the pages of the album and stopped at a photo taken at the couple's fiftieth wedding anniversary.

In the margin, John Scordo had written:

Just think about it for a minute. 50 big years. It was a very special day for us. Holy cow, 50 years—I don't remember being single. I think I was born married.

I must say, my wife is still a very beautiful girl.

ANOTHER SCRAPBOOK is filled with memories more bittersweet.

John Scordo's father died when he was an infant; his mother remarried but died shortly after the birth of John's half-brother, George. He was raised by an aunt and his grandmother.

During the Depression he worked as a teenager for the American Beauty bakery—not so much for the pay as for food to take home. He worked for a while in the weather department at Stapleton Airport but said he was forced to leave his job. His boss, he said, "didn't like Italians."

During World War II, John Scordo was stationed on Guam when he received a telegram informing him that his youngest brother's plane was shot down over Austria. Six hours later he received another telegram, which said his other younger brother was killed in the Pacific.

"I remember the pain of that, the excruciating despair of my aunt Carmie driving down to Western Union to pick up the telegrams," Mazone said. "He had had so many losses in his life, and it wasn't very easy, although he accepted his charge willingly."

After returning to Denver, John Scordo moved in with his wife and her parents and helped care for both of the elders until their deaths.

The couple then focused on each other.

"He obviously wanted to enjoy life through my brother (John II) and I," George Scordo said. "But the driving force was to take care of her."

EIGHT YEARS AGO began a period for which there is no photo album.

"After she was diagnosed with Alzheimer's, he took care of her for as long as he could," Scordo said.

As her health deteriorated, John suffered two heart attacks that led to open heart surgery, and he was forced to admit that he could no longer care for Carmella. After she moved to a nursing home, he visited her every day.

Despite a bout with Hodgkin's disease, he rarely changed his routine.

"He'd get up at 6:15 a.m., make coffee, and then clean the house from top to bottom. It was so clean that when you walk in the kitchen, your feet squeak," said Westerkamp, their neighbor. "He said, 'I want that house to look as nice for her when she comes home as when she left it.' He was waiting for her to come back."

Westerkamp paused.

"He knew she wasn't coming back."

As the disease progressed, everything faded from Carmie Scordo's recognition—everything except the sound of her husband's voice.

"At the very end, I'm not so sure that she recognized him, but she recognized his voice always," George Scordo said.

"It was very difficult to see them together for the last time on the day that she died. He said goodbye to her, he said that he still loved her, and that he was going to miss her. He said that he missed her now."

THE NIGHT AFTER HIS WIFE'S DEATH, John Scordo sat down with his sons.

"He said he was glad to have fulfilled his wishes, to take care of his wife, to outlive her, and make sure everything was taken care of," George Scordo said.

"Then he said, 'I don't think we had more than four arguments during those sixty years.'"

Four days later, the day after Valentine's Day, John Scordo was sitting comfortably in his chair when he began to speak softly.

"He said, 'It's been quite a life. It's been a wonderful life,'" George Scordo said. "With that, he took a deep breath, and he died.

"I think she was calling him," Scordo said and then smiled. "Or he was calling her."

'Loopie' Grows Up

Spc. Travis W. Anderson

As THE TOWN OF HOOPER streamed into the dirt streets for the funeral of the boy they loved and cursed, two women stood at their gas station, unfolding a brand new American flag.

"We need to do it at half-mast, JoDene," Pat Stoops said as her sister hoisted the flag, which immediately caught the wind.

"A man came in and gave us that flag the other day after he heard what happened," JoDene Ireland said. "He said we needed one."

They watched the flag, then looked over the Two Sisters cafe and gas station, where the boy they were about to bury had kept them laughing.

"We haven't closed since I've been here," Ireland said. "We had to close for this. I loved him like he was one of my own."

Sunday morning along Colorado Highway 17, by the gas station, cars sped down the road. Some headed for the nearby tourist sites in this part of the San Luis Valley: Great Sand Dunes National Park and Preserve, the Colorado Gator Farm and Reptile Park and, farther down the road, the UFO Watchtower.

Most cars, however, turned in at the lowered flag at the Two Sisters gas station, headed for the funeral of a young man who made the entire valley his playground.

From there, the cars filed past a trailer home set on three hundred acres of farmland where Travis Anderson and his family raised cattle and sheep before the drought claimed it all. There, a single mother struggled for nearly three decades to bring up five children.

It's the place where two men in Army uniforms showed up on the porch May 13, 2005, and Barbara Anderson refused to let them in.

THE DAY BEFORE THE FUNERAL for Army Spc. Travis W. Anderson, six men sat at the table inside the Anderson homestead, figuring they might as well start the story of Anderson's life on the day he was born, when the kid they still call "Loopie" got his nickname.

"At the hospital in La Jara, they mixed him up with another baby," said Dan Curtis, who was the closest to a father figure Travis Anderson ever had. "They kept bringing this other baby into Barbara's room, but she kept saying 'That's not my baby. That's not my baby.' "

When the nurses realized the mistake, the story goes, they went into another room to retrieve baby Travis. On his wrist, his incorrect bracelet read "Lupe," and the name stuck. Before they brought him back to his mother, the other mom already had begun nursing him.

"I like to say it was the first time he ate down at the neighbor's house," Curtis said, as those seated at the kitchen table burst into laughter.

At the table, Anderson's best friend looked up.

"I know something that I could say," Clifton Curtis said, and then hung his head, unable to speak.

"It's OK, Big Dog," said Tracey Freel, Anderson's uncle, thumping Clifton Curtis on the back. "We've all been there."

When the men managed to speak, the stories came in drawls —stories about the throngs of children he taught to hunt and how, later in life, he sent his entire paycheck to his family to help buy school supplies for his brother Buddy.

They talked about how he could make friends in a minute and recounted his instinctual shooting skills, showing off a photo of him at four years old, holding his first kill: two cottontail rabbits. They continued to talk about the coyotes, deer and elk he shot with stunning accuracy.

That's about when Dan Curtis realized that some of the most important stories hadn't been told.

"Now all this sounds like he was a saint. But he was also a mean, ornery little shit," Curtis said, to nods all around the table. "So, OK, who's going to tell the story?"

They looked at each other, knowing exactly what he was talking about, wondering if they should start down that road, since they all knew where it would lead.

AT THE TABLE, THEY BEGAN AGAIN, this time starting with the first time Travis ran away, when he was in kindergarten, and disappeared from school with another five-year-old, placing the whole town on alert as police and others scoured the area.

"I found them in an abandoned house," Freel said. "One of them still had his Teddy bear. They said they didn't like that school and were running away. I asked them how they were going to find anything to eat. They said they would hunt and fish."

The second time he ran away was hardly as innocent. At about fourteen years of age, Travis and the same friend slipped away from a baby sitter and drove all the way to New Mexico before they were caught stealing gas. When police caught up to them, Travis grabbed a gun and fired out the window.

"The judge asked him why he was shooting at the state patrolman, and Travis said he wasn't shooting at him, he was shooting at the tires—he said that if he was aiming at the patrolman he would be dead," Freel said.

Though he managed to avoid serious jail time, Anderson quit school not long afterward, following the death of his best friend in a car accident—a blow that sent him into a deep depression. He left home, working as a farmer and ranch hand from Montana to Nevada, but he always returned to the San Luis Valley and the high lakes in the mountains he knew since childhood.

Still, his family said, he lived much of that time "as if he didn't care."

It wasn't until after the September 11 terrorist attacks that he decided something had to change. He started that change by enlisting in the Army.

For once I feel like I'm doing the right thing, he wrote in a letter to his older sister, Toscha Alcorta. *I have made a lot of decisions in my life — some good, some bad, but nevertheless I've made it this far. I don't know what the future holds for me but no matter what I am ready.*

I'm tired of being a (screw-up).

BEFORE ENLISTING, Anderson faced one major hurdle: The military wouldn't take him without a high school diploma. At 26, he headed back to the place he spent much of his life trying to avoid.

"He was kind of embarrassed at going back to school when he was that old," his brother Buddy said. "But he did it. He wanted it."

After graduation, Anderson figured he had his life straight. Then one day he couldn't get out of bed. By the time he was diagnosed with Hantavirus, it was nearly too late.

"When they put him on the (medical) plane to Albuquerque, they said there was a 75 percent chance he would die before they landed," Dan Curtis said. "But he came back. He went from a 100-pound weakling to six-foot-four and 240 pounds."

Upon his return from basic training everyone noticed a marked change in the kid who suddenly held his shoulders high and dedicated himself to everything he started, shouting out his chores in military cadences.

"He was different," Buddy Anderson said. "He was proud."

At the table, the man whom he considered his father made a fist.

"That's what gets us," Curtis said, his voice shaking. "This kid had finally grown up. We had just gotten him into a full-fledged goddamn MAN, and then we lost him.

"That's what kills us all, right there."

WHEN THE STRANGE CAR pulled up on Friday the 13th, Barbara Anderson was immediately on alert.

"You know how country folk are," she said. "When they didn't park in the driveway, I knew something was wrong."

She watched the men walk around to her mother's home next door and wondered if she should call the police. Then she saw the uniforms.

"I knew. I knew immediately," she said. "I closed the door and turned off the light. I just didn't want them to come in and tell me."

Still, they came.

"They asked very nicely if they could come in, and I told them no," she said. "I don't know. I guess it's just mother's instinct. If they didn't come in, it wouldn't happen."

After hearing the commotion, her mother came over and convinced Barbara Anderson to let the men inside. In the next few days, the family learned how a car bomb hit Travis Anderson's Humvee, killing him and injuring several other soldiers.

To the troops in Bravo Company, Specialist Anderson wasn't known as "Loopie." In Iraq, he was "Cowboy," the kid who ended up as the heartbeat of his unit.

"Sometimes I wish we had a whole platoon of him," said Staff Sergeant Jeremy Schultz, who had served with Anderson but was home from Iraq after being wounded.

"I get goose bumps talking about him," Schultz said, raising his thick arm to prove it.

Many of the soldiers from his company traveled from Fort Stewart, Georgia, to honor Anderson. Once in Hooper, they met the large proportion of San Luis Valley kids who ended up in Iraq and saw the hardworking families with maps of Iraq tacked to their walls. They read the boxes of cards and condolences stacked in the Anderson home, some of them addressed simply, "To Loopie's Mom."

"You come down here, and you see all this — you see where he came from," Schultz said. "Now I know why he fit right in."

THE POPULATION OF HOOPER is 123. On Sunday, the gym at the elementary school swelled to nearly 600.

Inside, they started the memorial service with some of Anderson's favorite songs: the theme from *The Dukes of Hazzard*, Roger Miller's "Can't Rollerskate in a Buffalo Herd" and a slew of military marches. Friends and family told stories the way Anderson once did: stories involving big animals and big laughs, stories that may or may not have been altogether true.

Then a brigadier general rose to present the awards that Anderson never received, along with a few more that stunned the crowd.

"This is a family that understands sacrifice to this nation, a family that understands duty, honor and sacrifice," said Brigadier General Robert Reese, who traveled from White Sands, New Mexico.

He then presented a Bronze Star to Dan Curtis, the man who watched over Anderson most of his life but never received his own medals after the Vietnam War. Another Bronze Star went to Anderson's grandmother, recognizing the service of Anderson's grandfather, Jearold Freel, who fought in World War II but never received the honor.

The last Bronze Star went to the man who finally decided he was tired of being a screw-up.

After the service ended, Anderson's coffin was followed by its honorary pallbearer: Anderson's dog, Daniel.

As he climbed in the car on the way to the cemetery, Curtis looked over at the hearse.

"Well," he said, "I hope to hell we never have to do that again."

INSIDE THE TINY RITO ALTO CEMETERY northeast of Moffat, in the shadow of the Sangre de Cristo Mountains, Curtis looked at the headstones, at all the old names that would have recognized the newest one.

"There's old Mitchell," he said, pointing to a grave. "That ol' guy was drinking beer with Loopie right before he died. ... Half these people in here have been mad at 'im. But they still liked 'im."

In his pocket, Curtis carried the Bronze Star awarded to him at the funeral. As he walked along the graves, he thought back to the family's military service.

"I guess we just used up all our luck. When you're in some of these places, in some of these battles, you need all the luck you can get. I guess we just burned all our luck up. And there wasn't enough for Loopie."

Together, the mourners made their way to a special gravesite.

"We picked it out because it was covered with elk tracks and deer (droppings)," Tracey Freel said. "We put him right where the bucks will stand on his grave."

Once the burial honors began, the honor guard from Fort Carson fired a rifle salute and a herd of elk scattered in the distance. After the service, an old hunting buddy from Del Norte placed a coyote skin on the casket, which was also soon covered with flowers.

When the service was over, not everyone went home.

"As soon as I heard about this, I knew I wanted to bury my

brother," said Buddy Anderson, as he grabbed a shovel and a long-neck beer. "I didn't want someone to come in with a backhoe and fill him in. This is the most important day in my life. I need this to honor him."

Inside the empty cemetery, a dozen of Anderson's closest friends—some of them still dressed in their funeral clothes, some of them in their combat fatigues—also grabbed shovels, tossing soil and huge rocks back into the grave. The cemetery was soon filled with three of Travis Anderson's favorite smells: dirt, sweat, and beer.

Halfway through, they stopped.

"Let's have a toast," Buddy said, cracking open another one. Atop the half-filled grave, they tossed a set of antlers, then a rabbit call.

Before they could start digging, Dan Curtis fished a small case out of his pocket.

"Wait," he said, pulling out the medal he had just received, and tossed it into the grave. "Let's give him another Bronze Star."

As the dirt fell again, Curtis raised his bottle.

"Happy hunting, Loop," he said. "Happy hunting."

Quittin' Time

Wesley Denis Conda

ACROSS THE STREET FROM WHERE he was born, the last coal miner to leave town lay in a homemade coffin on his back porch.

"Wesley D. and Robbie Frances Conda," reads the sign at the front of the property. *"The Condarosa."*

From his stoop here behind the house in the tiny town of Marshall, south of Boulder, Wes Conda could point to the hill that once held the old two-room schoolhouse he attended. In another direction, he could point to the mines he knew—the ones he could find on the paths above ground and in miles of tunnels below.

As people gathered for his funeral service, one of his great-grandchildren brought a violin up near the casket and played the first notes of "Amazing Grace." Somebody pressed "play" on the tape deck, and Johnny Cash took it from there, followed by Loretta Lynn singing "Coal Miner's Daughter."

"With Wes's passing, an era is passing. A proud era, and one that many people today will know nothing about," said Jean Scott, chaplain of Hospice of Boulder County, who counseled Conda and his family during his last weeks. "There will be fewer and fewer people who will be able to say, 'I am the son—or daughter—of a coal miner.'"

Above the compound of family houses where they all gathered, his son Nick Conda stood at the same old steam whistle that used to blow at the mines around the area. He blasted the whistle three bursts in a row, the signal for quittin' time.

Wesley Denis Conda died of pancreatic cancer on May 10, 2002, at home. He was eighty-six.

FROM CONDA'S BACKYARD, his eighty-six-year-old cousin Wilbert Hale pointed to a hill a few miles away from the Conda house; he was really pointing at what was inside the hill.

"He worked up at the High View (mine) for a good long time. He was top-notch at running the punchin' machine," Hale said, referring to the massive jackhammer-like device that cut coal in the mines. "His old man ran the punching machine, too."

Though the Conda family owned the mine, that didn't mean its members were excused from the work—mostly digging "low coal" in small tunnels on their knees.

In many ways, Conda's life was as tough as the work: his mother died when he was nine years old; his brother later died of black lung disease. He made it through eighth grade in the tiny Marshall school where he wasn't known as a bully but wasn't one to be messed with. That was a trait that continued throughout his life: Like many of the Conda men, he was built like one of those coal-punching machines. And he could punch back.

In 1934, he met a woman as strong as he was but who could coax from him a softer side. With her Cherokee lineage, Robbie Frances Adams had endured her own share of difficult times. She had hiked with her brother from Tennessee to Colorado when she met Wes. They remained together for the next sixty-seven years.

"I walked 1,800 miles to get that man," she said, "and after I got him I wasn't going to give him up."

After nearly twenty-five years in the coal mines, Conda helped mine gravel to build the Boulder Turnpike (U.S. 36), then spent his time working at several clay mines and operating the family rock quarry on Eldorado Mountain until his retirement in 1975. Nearly two decades later, the family sold the mine to the city of Boulder Open Space, which began an ongoing restoration project.

After Conda's burial at Green Mountain Cemetery in Boulder, a few of the old-timers who returned for Conda's funeral stood in their bib overalls, looking over the old Marshall School photos, telling stories of close calls in the mines. Meanwhile, cyclists in day-glo spandex pedaled up the road.

"People see the statue of that miner in (nearby) Louisville and don't even know what it's for," one of the men said.

"There aren't any miners around here now," said Hale, who moved away a few years ago. "The ground is here, but the atmosphere's changed."

NOBODY IS SURE WHEN they started calling the family property the Conderosa—the place had similarities to the old homestead on

"Bonanza," and Wes Conda had more than a few things in common with the television patriarch, Bud Cartwright.

"He was always our leader," said his daughter, MaryFrances Moon. "Even in his last minutes he was leading us."

Of his eight children, six of them stayed on the property in Marshall, periodically adding houses, building the Conda compound.

"There was a magnet that kept us all here," said daughter Grace Bullock.

"It must just have been love, that's all I can figure," Frances Conda said, as the grown children gathered around. "It had to be, didn't it, kids?"

The same family members—nearly one hundred of them— visited Wes as he lay dying. Then—with the tools he had given them—they all pitched in to build his coffin.

"Even the smallest grandchildren helped," Moon said. "There were all these little hands with sandpaper, just rubbing away."

Lining the coffin was a handmade quilt depicting twelve red roses surrounded by forget-me-nots. Each family member made a stitch in the quilt.

If it weren't for that family presence, the patriarch likely would have died more than a decade ago when, during one of the couple's many trips to Las Vegas, Conda was violently mugged, leaving him unable to walk or speak. Slowly, the family nursed him back to health, and, even though he never fully regained his speech, they could still understand him. The grandkids felt the weight of his stare if they disobeyed; as always, they knew that if they walked in the house with a hat on, they had to put a dollar in a jar.

Grandson Robert Bullock remembers one word in particular.

"WATCH," he repeated. "If you heard that word, you knew to step out of the way. He was going to show you how it's done."

After the funeral, the grandchildren, great-grandchildren, and great-great-grandchild found new meaning in the word, as they brought shovels and a young pear tree to a piece of property north of the house and began to dig.

Before they planted the tree in the spot where the old man always looked out from the porch, one of the grandchildren's wives, Amy Bullock, dropped one of Conda's heavy black work shoes in the hole.

"When you do this, it's supposed to help the tree grow," she said.

"It gives the roots something to hold onto."

Swan Song for a Pioneer

Harold H. Gray

THE DAY BEFORE HE REACHED his final goal in life, Harold Gray sat in a hospital wheelchair, preparing for what would be his last day out.

At 104 years old, he was blind, nearly deaf, and could no longer walk. A few days earlier he had almost died of pneumonia but managed to pull through.

"He doesn't say much anymore, but he knows what's going on," said his son, Stan Gray, 76, before he entered the hospital room on the eve of his father's 105th birthday.

"He was pretty philosophical yesterday. He told me, 'I've had a really good life.' He was just ... summarizing. He never said anything about (death), but I think he knows he's in the home stretch."

Sometime around his one hundredth birthday, Harold Gray set a goal to live to 105. At the time, nobody knew why.

As it turned out, those last several years were just as important as all of those that came before.

In many ways, they were the most important of all.

For his first century of life, Harold Gray was known as a pioneer in the eastern plains town of Brush, where he started his career selling Model T Fords and ended up helping to shape the community as president of several economic development boards and as an active entrepreneur until he was ninety-three. In the process of achieving his accomplishments, however, the business almost always came first.

In those last years of his life—as he neared his goal of 105—he concentrated on his family in a way he never had in the past. In the process, he grew closer to his daughters and grandchildren (and great-grandchildren and great-great grandchildren). During that time he also found a new relationship with his only son, for whom he previously never seemed to have time.

To ACCOMPANY IT ALL, the man who had never been outwardly affectionate started to do something nobody expected.

He began to sing.

"None of us had ever heard him sing like that before. It started right about when he turned one hundred, and the older he got the more he sang," Stan said. "He drew strength from it, he told us that."

He mined most of his songs from the early twentieth century, many of them likely sung to him by his mother. Most of them were something he rarely was: undeniably sentimental.

Inside the hospital room on January 29, 2006, Stan Gray adjusted his father's sport coat and tie. A few blocks away, the congregation at the Methodist Church prepared for an early birthday celebration.

"Here's a song for you," Harold said, and began in a warbling tenor.

> *When it's springtime in the Rockies*
> *I'll be coming back to you*
> *Little sweetheart of the mountains*
> *with your bonny eyes of blue*
> *Once again I'll say I love you while*
> *the birds sing all the day*
> *When it's springtime in the Rockies*
> *In the Rockies, far away*

After his son straightened his tie and suit jacket, Harold Gray stared ahead through cloudy eyes.

"One hundred and five years old, and I don't look a day over forty," he said, his jowly face managing a smirk.

"One hundred and five years," he said a few minutes later. "That's enough."

Harold Holton Gray died February 11, 2006, in Brush. He was 105.

HAROLD GRAY AND HIS FAMILY arrived in the Brush area—about ninety miles northeast of Denver—in 1910, traveling from Loveland in a horse-drawn buggy.

"*At the time when I was born, and history will affirm this, there were no televisions, radios, credit cards, nor airplanes: the list goes on,*" he said in an autobiography he dictated to his daughter, Carolyn Thornsby, in 1998, when he was ninety-seven years old.

The manuscript—which he called "Gray Matter"—was written the way he spoke: clipped and stoic, interspersed with historical tales of the area, punctuated with deadpan humor.

"When you get to this age you don't have a lot of peers," Harold said when he was 103, *"but you also don't have to worry about peer pressure."* On his 104th birthday, he joked, *"If I knew I'd live this long, I'd have taken better care of myself."*

That easygoing, straightforward personality earned him the title of "Dean of the Brush Businessmen" from a local newspaper, and "Outstanding Pioneer" by the Brush Rodeo Association. At Brush High School athletic events, where the official mascot is the "Beetdiggers," the 1918 alum took pride as the oldest Beetdigger alive.

While he concentrated on business interests that ranged from car dealerships to a horse racetrack, he rarely had time for family. Even when he was home, he later admitted, he was emotionally distant with his children.

Looking back, his daughters just figured that's the way he was—filled with traditional values, following in the "grand old man" footsteps of his father, and probably his father before.

"While we may not have had the contemporary view of constant closeness and warm fuzzies, he provided a model for us, of being a genteel, positive, witty man," said his youngest daughter, Cynthia Gray. "And the function of somebody modeling those things on a day-to-day basis is a gift. It's worth a lot."

Though all of his children say their childhood was happy— with a laugh-track primarily provided by their mother—Stan Gray would later lament that his father never found time to toss a ball to him or attend a single athletic event, that for the bulk of his life, he was "emotionally absent."

As his father neared his last goal, they spent nearly every day together, making up for lost time, wondering when it would finally run out.

AT THE BRUSH CEMETERY, the headstone marked GRAY has been etched with Harold's name on it for more than a decade—ever since they buried his wife, Doris, and he swore to remain nearby.

Occasionally, Harold would return to the cemetery, to talk with his wife about the times they shared—and times they missed. During one visit, he sang his favorite song to her—a 1920s standard called "Together."

> *She's gone from me*
> *But in my memories*
> *We always will be*
> *Together*

For his funeral, he requested they sing a reprise.

On February 15, 2006, dozens of family members and friends gathered in the cemetery, where they read the inscription on the back of the headstone—a marble marker Harold designed.

The headstone is etched with a picture of the home the family has occupied since 1927. Underneath, the stone reads simply, "MEMORIES."

"We're burying a lot of history today," a friend said, as he stood near two of Harold's daughters, Corinne White and Carolyn Thornsby.

"We won't forget," Carolyn said.

After most of the mourners left, Stan's daughter, Carrie Gray, walked to the casket and pulled off a flower. "Could you get me one, too?" Stan asked, and she handed him a huge yellow blossom.

In the biting wind, he took the flower, and placed it in his lapel.

THREE WEEKS BEFORE HAROLD DIED, Stan found the strength to tell his father something he had never said before—something that, even two years ago, remained too uncomfortable to utter.

In 1997, Stan agreed to move in with his father after the family realized that Harold could no longer live alone. Though Stan still resented the emotional distance he felt from his father, he says he never lost his respect for the old man and felt an obligation to care for him—a sense of responsibility he credits to his mother's upbringing.

For the next seven years the two men lived together in the same home where Harold spent nearly eighty years. As Harold's sight and mobility waned, Stan wound up providing care. He devised innovative ways to get them closer. Some days, they drove around dusty country roads, listening to Rockies baseball games. Some evenings, they drove to a special point on the plains to watch sunsets together, with Stan describing the colors for his blind father.

Still, in 2004 he admitted, "We're good friends. We're not ... we're not affectionate in any way. ... There's no bond of brotherhood.

"I know this sounds hard, but we're not close."

Two years later, just before his father reached his final goal in life, a few days before that 105th birthday, Stan reached a goal of his own.

By then, he had continued to grow closer to his father. Even after a nasty fall put Harold in a nursing home in 2004, Stan continued to visit, occasionally even bringing a bottle of beer to split between the two of them.

Then one night two weeks ago, as his father lay weak in the hospital, he realized he had something to say.

"I wondered, 'How much is it going to hurt to tell him?'" he said. "But those three words, you have to mean it and feel it before you say them ...

"So I finally said it, for the first time in my life. I finally got the guts up and told him that I loved him."

Inside the old home on Everett Street, he looked down at the table and smiled.

"He told me he wanted to thank me. And he said he'd had loving thoughts about me, too."

Stan shook his head.

"I wondered so long about how hard it would be to say that," he said. "And you know what?

"It was easy."

HAROLD GRAY'S FINAL BIRTHDAY celebration began the same place his funeral would take place twelve days later: at the Brush United Methodist Church—a building he helped construct.

Though he was recovering from a bout with pneumonia, he insisted on traveling to the church to see the newest addition: an elevator to make it wheelchair-accessible.

As he arrived, church members held the elevator door for Harold, waiting for him for the inaugural ride.

When the elevator door opened to the church's community room, he was greeted with strains of "Happy Birthday" and a lapful of greeting cards.

"I am honored," he said. "I feel privileged."

After returning to the hospital that day, Stan placed a piece of pumpkin pie—another birthday request—on the nightstand.

"All right, Dad, we'll be heading off, now."

"One more song," his father said.

As Stan and the nurses gathered around, he began again:

> *There are smiles that make us happy,*
> *There are smiles that make us blue,*
> *There are smiles that steal away the teardrops,*
> *As the sunbeams steal away the dew*
> *Here are smiles that have a tender meaning,*
> *That the eyes of love alone may see ...*

As he tried to finish the song, Harold's eyes glassed over and his voice cracked, unable to finish the last verses:

> *And the smiles that fill my life with sunshine*
> *Are the smiles that you give to me.*

Stan bent over to his father's ear.

"That's all right, Dad," he said, as he turned to leave. "That sounded real good."

'Your Life Must Be So Dull'

Severin David Foley

DEPENDING ON HIS MOOD or the time of day, the crusty old man on the park bench might brush a hand through his enormous, filthy gray beard and tell passers-by about his life as a Benedictine monk. While keeping an eye on a shopping cart filled with his only possessions, the artist, scholar, and priest in the funky homemade clothes would sing in flawless Latin.

He could quote obscure Russian novels and cite esoteric philosophy but could also describe the way a carburetor works or the intricacies of horse saddles through the centuries.

Then Severin Foley would say something to ruin everything. He always did.

"Incorrigible." "An old coot." "Belligerent." "Misogynist." These are the words that even his friends and family use to describe the Denver native. They also say that he was absolutely, undeniably brilliant.

Severin David Foley died June 23, 2002, of complications from a stroke. He was seventy-six.

"He always said, 'Adventure is merely inconvenience rightly considered,'" says former college friend John Atlee, one of the few people to put up with Foley for more than one day.

"It was inconvenient when it meant dealing with Sev," Atlee says. "But oh, oh, it was one hell of an adventure."

THE ANTAGONISM TOWARD Severin began before he was born. The first child in an already shaky marriage, he was the immediate object of his father's frustration. William Foley never really spoke to his son until Severin was thirteen years old.

"That's important because it left a scar on Severin," says his brother, Litmer, who lives in Loveland.

"He grew up with an aversion to authority figures of any kind. It's unfortunate, because it got in the way of his accomplishing all that he could have. Everything he got into, he self-destructed."

He found encouragement from his mother, Grace, and an aunt, who praised his interests in art and music, but few others seemed to understand his frustrating quest for knowledge. He attended Cathedral High School but preferred to skip class in favor of the lakeside at City Park, where he would memorize encyclopedias. His brother says he saw an IQ test where Severin scored 152.

"He could talk about any subject not only in depth, but in currency," Litmer Foley says. "It was just the business of life where he was a misfit."

Severin Foley eventually joined the Benedictine Order at Holy Cross Abbey in Canon City. It wasn't exactly the best place to avoid authority figures. After continuously challenging the abbot, he was transferred to Conception Abbey, in Missouri, where he took his vows as a Benedictine monk and was ordained as a Catholic priest. He taught seminary school there for the next two decades but was eventually expelled after continual run-ins with the abbot.

"Not only was he a challenge, but he also challenged everything," says Atlee, who met Severin while studying at the University of Oklahoma. The monks had ostensibly sent Severin to the university to study art, but, more likely, the monks were trying to get him out of their hair, he says.

"He questioned everyone and everything. He questioned the church. ... He questioned life itself. He charged it head on with lance in hand balanced on the steed of his beliefs," Atlee says. "Did it ever matter that it was a windmill or a monastery? I don't think so."

Foley joined a street ministry in Oklahoma and lived with his new congregation, on the pavement. He celebrated high Mass in parks, using a paper cup for a chalice. He performed marriages and baptisms on street corners.

"For all of the thirty-five years I have known him, I never questioned his belief in God," Atlee says. "I have questioned his belief in the Catholic Church ... but his faith could not be questioned."

He moved to San Francisco and lived on the streets and in subsidized housing thanks to help from his brother and a welfare check. He proceeded to antagonize every landlord he met, piling his homes full of magazines, newspapers, and various trinkets and junk, sometimes all the way to the ceiling.

He relished the inevitable court trials that would come after each eviction notice. It didn't matter that he lost every case and was often thrown out of court. He was also tossed from government aid offices and several nursing homes. He chalked the evictions to victories since he refused to cave on his principles. Whenever someone tried to have him tested for mental problems, he reverted to his knowledge of psychiatry and faked his way through the interview.

"He alienated just about everyone he ever met, except maybe me," Atlee says. "I guess I was lucky he never lived with me. It may have been the salvation of our friendship."

AT HIS HOME IN LOVELAND, Litmer Foley sits at the table where his brother often criticized his "conservative" lifestyle but also where the two had deep conversations about everything and nothing.

Throughout the years, Litmer invited his brother back to Colorado for vacations, where the mountains were one of the few places he seemed to find solace. When Severin found trouble, his brother would help bail him out. When Severin returned to Colorado in 2001, his brother cared for him.

As he read through stacks of rambling, ranting letters and screeds sent by his brother, Litmer Foley considered the question that so many people have asked over the years.

Why support a man who was so ungrateful?

"It's kind of ironic," Foley says. "After watching Severin, I decided very early on that I didn't want to be like him. So the irony is that my brother is responsible for the very behavior that he was criticizing." The very behavior he needed to depend on.

After his brother's death, Litmer Foley was surprised to receive dozens of condolences from around the country—people who, despite Severin Foley's attempts to push them away, found a kind of enlightenment from the man who never stopped challenging them to think.

"*I do not wish for another life,*" Severin wrote in one of the letters to his brother, "*other than to look for each change and adventure and to enjoy it, cope with it, knowing that nothing will last or be finished, and that I don't ever need to compromise.*"

He ended the letter the same way he always began, the same way he lived, insisting on the last word.

Your life must be so dull,
　— Severin.

'I Was Only Nineteen. Why Me?'

Orlando B. Trujillo

ALONE FOR TWO DAYS IN THE PACIFIC OCEAN, Orlando Trujillo was kept afloat by a life jacket. The pounding waves had ripped off most of his clothes, along with a layer of skin. His head baked in the pounding sun, while his body shivered in the water. He had only been in the Navy for six months. He was nineteen years old.

"Over and over, I repeated my prayers, and when the hours dragged on and I continued to go under and still come up, I became sick and discouraged," he later told the *Catholic Register.* *"Way down under the water 40 or 50 feet it was black, dark, my head was splitting and I swallowed a great deal of water. When my head was above the water I threw up constantly."*

Hours earlier, on December 19, 1945, his destroyer, the USS *Hull,* had sunk in a typhoon off the Philippines—a storm that also claimed two other destroyers of the renowned Third Fleet. After escaping from the sinking ship, Trujillo was tossed into waves taller than any building he had seen back home in Denver.

After the storm, a naval ship sailed past without spotting him. He screamed and waved to no avail when aircraft flew overhead. He thought of giving up.

"All I would have had to do was slip out of that life suit and my troubles would have been over in a matter of seconds," he told the *Register.*

"Somebody at home must have been praying for me."

When he finally saw a ship approaching, he saw soldiers shooting machine guns into the water and thought it must be a Japanese ship, aiming for him. As the ship approached, he realized it was friendly. The American soldiers onboard were shooting at sharks.

After forty-nine hours in the water, Trujillo was one of only about three hundred men rescued from the sunken ships, which took nearly eight hundred soldiers to the bottom of the ocean.

"For years, my Dad wondered, 'Why me? Why did God save me?'" said Danny Trujillo. "He said, 'There were men there with families, men with children. I was only nineteen. Why me?'"

From her home on 23rd Street in downtown Denver, Mildred Romero was devastated to hear that the *Hull* had sunk. She had been thinking more about the Trujillo boy, who had grown up only a block away. They had attended school and church together, and dated on occasion. She prayed for him. She wondered if he still had a girlfriend.

"I saw him when he came home on survivor's leave," she said. "We started going out. We went out for a long time, and then one day I told him I was going to get married soon. 'To who?' he asked, and I said 'I don't know, but I'm going to get married this year.'

"A week later he proposed."

After the war, Trujillo worked with the Denver Tramway for nearly a decade, but, as the couple began their family, his wife had another proposal for him.

"He loved to cook," she said. "I knew he could run a restaurant. I knew he could."

They found a little place on South Federal and named it Lolita's, after Mildred's mother.

Through the years, Orlando Trujillo was a staple at the restaurant, often providing entertainment as he cooked, singing songs from the 1940s loud enough for all the patrons to hear.

Inside and outside the restaurant, he shared more than his voice.

"He never turned anyone away. He always had food for people who couldn't afford it," said his son, Greg Trujillo. "There were times literally on a Friday or Saturday that the back of the restaurant looked like a soup line. I remember these guys once offering him their car battery if he'd give them a burrito. He said, 'Don't worry about it,' and he fed them."

As the restaurant prospered, his philanthropy continued, sometimes to the amazement of his eight children.

"I remember one time driving home with him and I was actually kind of angry," recalled Greg Trujillo. "I said, 'Dad, I can't understand why you would give away all this food, all this money.' He turned to me and said, 'What's it to you? Do you have everything you need? Why should you be concerned about this?'

"It really hit me. Man. It was just the generousness."

As he stood before hundreds of people gathered at St. Jude Church in Lakewood, Greg Trujillo remembered another of his father's lessons, one taught on one of the coldest nights of the year. "He asked us kids to gather up all our sleeping bags. He put them in the car and then went to Kmart and bought five more."

Earlier in the evening, Orlando Trujillo had seen a story on television about the homeless people from Denver gathering at Holy Ghost Church to get out of the below-zero weather. He drove his family to the church and gave away every sleeping bag.

"Then there was the time when his car was hit by a drunk driver," said Lonnie Trujillo, another son. "The police took the guy to jail. The guy didn't have insurance, he didn't have anything. My dad went to the store and bought three bags of groceries and took it over to their house, to the house of this guy's family. I remember just going, 'Dad, why would you do this?' He said, 'It's not his family's fault.'"

"Remember, that happened during Christmastime," Mildred Trujillo said. "So he also bought presents for the man's children."

After selling Lolita's, Trujillo opened the Bear Valley Inn inside the Bear Valley Shopping Center, which he co-owned until suffering a heart attack. Looking for a less stressful way of doing business, he opened a hot dog stand and parked it near the unemployment office.

"What did he end up doing?" his wife asked, laughing. "He gave away hot dogs."

During the late 1970s and 1980s, Trujillo and his hot dog cart were a fixture near Capitol Hill and at the annual People's Fair.

"In my opinion, he opened the stand for one reason: people. He liked people," Danny Trujillo said. "I remember one of his favorite phrases was, 'Pass it on. Pass on the kindness.'

"That's the way he was. Pass it on."

WHEN ORLANDO TRUJILLO was diagnosed with terminal heart disease, he took it in stride, confident in his faith, justifying his impending death with an encyclopedic knowledge of biblical verse and insight of his own.

"I wrote down a thought that I carry with me in my wallet," he wrote in a newsletter sponsored by Hospice of Metro Denver. *"It gives me the right perspective: 'Life and death are part of the same adventure. Do not fear to die and do not shrink from the joy of life.'"*

When he became involved with the hospice organization, health care workers told his family that it was common for dying people to begin seeing visions of people they knew who had died.

"They told us he would likely have 'visitors.' And he did," Mildred Trujillo said. "But some of them he didn't recognize."

When family and friends asked him who the mystery faces were, he thought for a few moments before responding.

"Well, the only reason I can figure out is that I pray for people when I see a flood, I pray for people in Beirut, I pray for people in Honduras," he told them. "I pray for people all over the world because there are so many people who have nobody to pray for them.

"And I think they come to visit me."

SHORTLY BEFORE HER HUSBAND'S DEATH, Mildred Trujillo purchased a compact disc filled with love songs. They rarely made it past the first song, called "Always."

"That song said everything about the love we had for each

other," she said. "When I put it on and we heard it, he and I cried. We would play it over and over."

Before his death, she put on the song for the last time.

"I had it on and I started to walk away. He said, 'I think I can dance with you now.'

"I went over, and we just swayed."

Orlando B. Trujillo died at home March 9, 1999. He was seventy-two.

DURING THE RECEPTION at St. Jude's, Danny Trujillo sat among the tears and stories falling from dozens of tables in the church and repeated the question his father asked for so long.

"For years, he asked, 'Why me? Why did God save me from the ocean?'

"As he grew older, he looked at his family, all the people he loved.

"He said, 'I know why.'"

The City's Last Cowboy Battled the New West

Laura 'Billie' Preston

THE OTHER DAY THEY BURIED BILLIE the way she told them to—with her boots on.

"She's wearing blue jeans, a beaded belt, and a beautiful cowboy shirt she wore when riding in the parades—black with red flowers," Maxine Jarrad said as she sat near her best friend's grave. "Her boots were black leather, trimmed in red."

Born in Oklahoma before it was Oklahoma, she lived in Aurora before it was Aurora. Her people were in the United States long before there were states. During nearly a century of life, she would teach the kids of Colorado what life could be like and remind the adults not to forget.

On top of her casket was draped a blanket embroidered with horses. She never saw that blanket, but she knew how it felt.

"Bill was blind by the time I gave (the blanket) to her," Jarrad said, "so she would ask me, 'What color's them horses?' and I'd tell her, 'Well, one's brown, one's white, one's got a red bridle.' She couldn't see them, but she pictured them."

Around her neck is something else she felt.

"Around her neck is a medicine bag," Jarrad said. "There's an eagle claw, little rocks, pebbles, and some dirt from her land."

"It's elements of life," said Jarrad's son, David McCann. "Elements of her life."

Laura "Billie" Preston died July 24, 2000, in Aurora. She was ninety-six.

AMONG THE FEW POSSESSIONS in her modest home is a cherished piece of paper enrolling Laura Jones "a citizen of the Cherokee Nation," stamped January 19, 1907. She said her great grandfather was a Cherokee chief, and as a child she danced for Teddy Roosevelt. Even when nearly everyone started calling Laura by a new name, she would remember the stories of her grandparents—stories of the terrors they faced, stories of the Trail of Tears—and Billie would remember how to repeat them. She quit school in the third grade to go to work, and she eventually took a job running an elevator in a nearby town.

"'Well,' she would tell people, 'I had my ups and downs,'" Jarrad remembered, laughing. "'I had my ups and downs,' she would say."

After the funeral Jarrad stood in her home, describing the first time she saw Billie Preston. It was 1950 and Jarrad was working in a Safeway store in Aurora. Preston hitched her horse to the front of the store and walked in, dressed as usual in overalls and a cowboy hat, ready to sell the store fresh eggs from her farm.

"The manager said, 'You see that person over there? If you look at her, you can't tell if she's a man or a woman, but she's got the biggest heart, and you'll never meet a better person,'" Jarrad said. "Over the next fifty years, I found out that was true."

She had come to Denver with her fiancé, Bryce Preston, and they married in 1924. The couple moved to Aurora, where Billie built a house while he served in the military. She learned to become more independent as he fell into bouts with alcoholism. He died in 1973, and she lived by herself for the next twenty-five years.

She rode her horse everywhere, prompting cowboys at the National Western Livestock Show to dub her "Bill." In the little house she built with her own hands, she rolled her own cigarettes from Bull Durham tobacco until she was ninety-one years old. She made sure her rolling papers were always free from glue—she was sure that's what gave people cancer. The only time anyone ever saw her wear a dress was at her mother's funeral.

"When I first met her, she was working on a coal truck, hauling coal and cleaning out furnaces. She worked like a man," Jarrad said. "At night, she would clean the bowling alley."

In her spare time she would ride her horse Patches down Colfax Avenue, collecting money to help build the famous "Gateway to the Rockies" sign that used to span Colfax near Potomac Street. She would scan the trash bins for toys and then refurbish them and donate them to underprivileged children. As she grew older and lost her sight, she would spend her time in classrooms and at the Aurora History Museum, painting oral portraits of life in a town the kids could no longer see.

"Billie honestly expressed her love for Aurora and how she was dealing with her blindness," said Betsy Lamb, who taught at Tollgate Elementary. "She hugged and spoke to every child she could touch. ... She made them all her grandchildren, finally numbering in the thousands."

From a scrapbook, Lamb found a collection of thank-you notes from the students.

"It must be neat to have a friend like Billie," one of the school kids wrote her. "Last night I told my parents all about the things she told us. They were surprised when I said I have a new grandma."

THE LEATHER ON BILLIE PRESTON's photo album was worn slick and soft as a comfortable saddle. On the front, red, childlike letters spelled out "PATCHY." Inside, she detailed a battle between the old West and the new.

It started back in the late fifties, when Aurora annexed her property at East 25th and Havana streets and rezoned it as residential land, restricting any livestock on the property. By then, her old mare Patches had been grazing there for years.

"Patches didn't come to Aurora," she once told the *Denver Post*. "Aurora came to her."

Instead of moving away, Billie Preston dug in. Soon, letters of support flooded her mailbox—and letters of outrage flooded the city's.

"*I firmly believe you are standing on your rights to try and keep your old trusty horse," wrote Col. Hall from Thermopolis, Wyoming, on an envelope bearing a 3-cent stamp.*

"*Bully for you and Patches, too!" wrote a woman from Ajo, Arizona. "True American individualism will surely disappear forever if a few like you don't fight for it.*"

Eventually, the City Council ruled against horses or livestock within the city limits—with the exception of Patches. The headlines in the next morning's paper read, "Aurora is now a one horse town."

TWO SILVER SIX SHOOTERS adorn the sides of Patches' bridle, which hangs at the front entrance to Jarrad's house. The old splotchy paint horse died on July 4, 1969, but her playground still exists near Preston's—one of the last remaining open places from the woman's famous stories. Preston eventually reconciled with the city and even donated her land to Aurora.

City officials have long since taken down the giant sign proclaiming Aurora "Gateway to the Rockies." These days, that part of Colfax is spanned by I-225, and the old Chamber of Commerce building nearby is now a Park-n-Ride. The "Gateway" sign lies in pieces at the Aurora History Museum, where they're trying to raise enough money to put it back up somewhere, someday.

"They've got some new sign, now," Lamb said at a gathering after the funeral. "It's got a sun or something on it."

"That's the City of Aurora logo," McCann said.

"Billie sure missed that old sign," Jarrad said. "She always hoped they'd put it back someday."

"Yeah, new things are not always good things," Lamb said.

"More importantly," McCann said, "old things are often the best things."

One Empty Seat at the Deli

Nicholas Papadakis

AS THE LUNCH CROWD FILLS the place they call The Deli, the only empty seat is the one with the best view.

The vacant chair is positioned near an old bench covered with shag carpeting, under descriptions of sandwiches that carry the names of the people who eat them: The Jimbo, The Don, The Ralph, The Tom (cheese 10¢ extra). For the past twenty-five years, that seat was reserved for a guy named Nick, who never thought to name a sandwich after himself.

"Tell Nick that Bo was in, OK?" a man tells the workers behind the counter, after seeing the empty chair. Another guy chimes in, "Tell Nick that I said hi, will ya?"

Inside The Deli that Nick and June Papadakis built in downtown Pueblo, construction workers sit with lawyers; cops eat with county secretaries. A ninety-year-old man comes in most every day, just as he has since the place opened. These customers are the first to admit they know "this old hole in the wall" too well, so it's tough to miss all that emptiness in the corner.

If Nick Papadakis heard a joke at 11:30 a.m., everyone on Main Street knew it by 1 o'clock, the punch line escorted by a deep belly laugh, powered by an unashamedly deep belly. As he sat in the chair with a view of the entire restaurant, he could match each face with a name and—more often than not—a sandwich. From his perch at the back of the restaurant, he pontificated and gesticulated, his gruff voice bellowing out opinions on sports, politics, and, most importantly, food.

For several weeks, the noontime crowd has known that Nick won't be there; most have heard about the sixty-four-year-old's fight with lung cancer. As they stream into the restaurant on August 2, however, few are prepared for the phone call.

"His kidneys are failing," Nick's daughter Michele Carpino says, after hanging up her cell phone, relaying a message from his hospice nurse: "It's only a matter of hours."

As the extended family closes the restaurant to return to his bedside, Nick's wife of forty-three years looks back at his chair.

"I don't know what we're going to do with it when he's gone," June Papadakis says. "There's just an empty space here. There's a hole."

NICHOLAS PAPADAKIS GREW UP around a melting pot of busy people and did his best to replicate both for the rest of his life. His father's family emigrated to San Francisco from Crete in the early 1900s, and his father eventually found a job operating one of the famous cable cars. Nick was soon riding alongside his father, ringing the bell, reveling in the attention.

He made the most of a poor upbringing with a slew of jobs—the most beneficial was at J.C. Penney, where he saw a girl named June Vincenti in the toy department one day and (as he would later say repeatedly) promptly swept her off her feet.

"He was pushing a toy cart and I was bending over and he pushed it right into me," June says. "He came over, picked me up, and we fell for each other."

They married in 1959, after Nick's tour in the Navy, and he began selling life insurance. In 1971 the couple and their two daughters, Alison and Michele, moved to Pueblo. Papadakis continued to sell insurance with various companies, but the two kept saying how much they missed a good delicatessen like the kind that dotted the Bay Area. Against everyone's advice, they decided to start their own.

"At the time, few people in Pueblo even knew what pastrami or pumpernickel was," June Papadakis says. "Once we got past that, they kept coming back."

While June and her sister, Linda Dorsey, along with the daughters, cooked and prepared sandwiches, Nick acted as maitre d', busboy, and order taker. Though he continued to sell insurance a few doors down, everyone could see that his true passion was everyone else's break time: the lunch rush.

"The first time you came into the deli, he memorized your name, so the second time you came in he wrote it on the pad without asking," Carpino says. He also kept a freezer full of ice cream cups that weren't for sale—he only doled them out free to children, guaranteeing new customers.

Away from The Deli, he loved to dance, whether it was Motown or Mantovani. He spent hours on crossword and computer games but reveled in food, especially sweets; he could reportedly smell doughnuts through walls. He also loved a good drink and made a mean martini, always with his own touch; after one thunderstorm, he made cocktails with the hailstones.

An extremely stubborn man, friends and workers eventually gave up telling him how to improve anything—they figured it was less trouble to do it Nick's way just to avoid the debate. But he was also known for his kindness. Several developmentally disabled men knew they could come in for a sandwich and conversation; he was also known to take leftover sandwiches to homeless men in a nearby alley. And it didn't end at the deli.

"One year at Christmas they decided not to give our family members any presents and instead spent all that money on a needy family," Carpino says.

"They said, 'We're not doing presents this year,'" she remembers. "They said, 'We're giving the gift of love.'"

ON THE AFTERNOON of August 2, 2002—fifteen hours before Nick Papadakis' death, he lies unconscious in his bed. He is bald and thin from chemotherapy; his massive hands rest on his slowly rising chest. The room is filled with photos of The Deli and of his family; as usual, he is surrounded by the regulars.

After several minutes inside his room, family members return to the kitchen, leaving June alone with her husband.

"When we first took him to the hospital, he would send us all out of the room at the end of the night so he and Mom could be alone," Carpino says. "She always got the last kiss."

A few minutes later, as the family tells stories in the kitchen, a voice crackles over an intercom linked to the bedroom. Nobody had realized the intercom was accidentally left on.

"I love you," June's voice says over the radio, calm and steady. "I love you. I love you. I love you."

Quietly, Carpino walks over to the intercom and clicks off the switch.

Choosing Life's Words
by Hand

Elaine Jorgensen Peck

IN A PLACE WHERE THE AIR smells like words, Tom Parson finds one of Elaine Peck's final poems. It weighs about ten pounds.

"This is one of the last things she printed," Parson says as he hefts out a block of lead letters set by her hand.

> *Lasso some laughter*
> *When troubles confound you*
> *Let love like an aura of*
> *Peace surround you*

These days, someone could type up the poem on a computer and print it out in seconds. For Elaine Peck, it meant choosing the letters individually from a wooden drawer and lining them up properly on the makeshift metal page, set in reverse. From there, the eighty-year-old woman would walk to one of the ancient half-ton machines and begin clacking away.

Inside his workshop in Denver where he now stores much of her collection of lead letters, pictures, and writings, Parson walks over to a century-old Chandler & Price printing press. He pushes the treadle with his foot and watches the enormous metal plate kiss the paper, just the way his mentor taught him. When he pulls out the paper, the ink is still fresh:

Ephemeral but precious forever
Elaine Jorgensen Peck
1916–2001

ELAINE PECK'S CHILDHOOD was punctuated by the sound of the letterpress. Her father started out as a "printer's devil" in 1890 at a newspaper in Brigham City, Utah, when he was fourteen. Elaine started when she was thirteen, in his printing shop in Salt Lake City, and ever since her hands were stained with ink.

Elaine's mother died when she was six, and Elaine remained very close to her father, working alongside him during the day at his print shop and taking classes at night to complete high school. Grades were never a problem—after all, she was always surrounded by words.

In a biography she wrote about her father, she hinted at the origin of her passion for letters and proper use of language. As her father lay dying in the hospital, two of the nurses were speaking to each other and one said, "He has false teeth, hasn't he?" With his dying word, he corrected her.

"Artificial," he said.

In the early 1950s, after selling her father's shop, Elaine married another printer, Jess Peck, and the couple moved to Denver.

In her pocket she carried a few pieces of brass—typesetting spacers from her father's old press.

As her husband worked the Linotype at the *Rocky Mountain News*, she worked as a proofreader at the *Denver Post* and various publishing houses while helping raise their two children. In her home workshop, under a portrait of fifteenth century printer Johann Gutenberg, her personal presses continued to run.

Shortly after arriving in Denver in 1953, she formed the Columbine Amateur Press Club, which fostered appreciation for the old letterpresses that were being quickly abandoned for new printing technology. Members of the group published their own writings—poems, random thoughts, printing hints—and mailed them to each other in packets.

Each publication—often only a single page—had its own title. Over the years, Peck's included: *"Peck's Patter," "Inklings"* (and its thinner cousin, *"Inklets"*), *"Miss Elaineous Photo Static,"* and *"Tiny Treasures Press."*

One Valentine's Day publication is covered with hearts and includes a message directly from hers:

"A dedicated printing craftsman hits the mark by putting heart into his art," she wrote. *"He accepts the challenge to create a thing of beauty."*

FROM A BUNDLE OF PECK'S publications, her former apprentice Gail Watson pulls out the piece of paper that started their friendship.

"I printed this BOOKMARK from movable type on a HANDPRESS at the Printing Extravaganza May 1, 2, and 3, 1985 Currigan Hall, Denver, Co."

Watson was visiting the exposition when she noticed the white-haired woman standing alone with her printing press.

"Everyone was rushing to the new technology, and here she was with this great old machine," Watson says. "A lot of people didn't have time to stop and see her because they were too busy running off to the 3M booth, to the future."

After Peck showed Watson how to print the bookmark, the pair formed a friendship and later earned a grant from the Colorado Council on the Arts master/apprentice program. It was one more accomplishment to add to a huge list.

A member of the National Amateur Press Association since 1936, Peck held several offices, including president. In 2000 she received one of the most prized awards in amateur printing: the Gold Composing Stick, handed out by a printers organization made up of historians and called, aptly enough, The Fossils. In handing her the award, the group noted her ability to interest people about the dying art of letterpress printing; more than that, to excite them.

"She was a mild-mannered woman with a steely will," Watson says. "It wasn't as if she was this forceful presence. It was more like the lunar pull."

In recent years Peck edited a newsletter for the Mormon Church, to which she belonged her whole life. She continued to print her poetry, much of it about love, printing, and her love of printing. For her, the process was like her poems—simple, tactile, and honest.

"I learned from her that you have to share what you know," Watson says. "To be passionate about something and to freely share that with the world. That's the most important thing."

NEAR THE THOUSANDS OF LETTERS in his home workshop, Tom Parson keeps a drawer of lead snowflakes. There are tiny metal images of flowers, animals, and elaborate etchings. Parson promises to keep these bits of Elaine Peck alive through the presses that his mentor taught him to appreciate.

"If you know what they are, they're enormous treasures," Parson says. "It's a wonderful connection. I feel connected to a whole string of history because of her."

Peck continued printing as long as her body would allow—until a stroke in the late 1990s. Once she moved to a nursing home she still helped edit a newsletter.

For her eighty-third birthday, friends held a party where the guests printed bookmarks on a letterpress. When she died November 28, at eighty-five, she was no longer able to stand at the press, but she had already written her last words. They come from a publication called *Tiny Treasures from the Tiny Treasures Press*. The type is called Goudy; the ink is Atlas Cowboy Blue. The words, as always, were selected by hand.

"*One of my earliest recollections is of 'helping' my father by standing some 48-point type up in the case when I was five,*" she wrote.

"*Probably one of my last memories of this life will not be far removed from our little world of letters.*"

Exploding Turkeys, Wieners, and Champagne

Robert L. Druva

THE RECIPE FOR DRUVA'S FAMOUS STUFFING appears on page 405 of the neighborhood cookbook, sandwiched between homestyle recipes for Chicken a la King and Cheesy Potato Bake. For Bob Druva, it was the perfect place to hide another grin.

"*This marvelous concoction was brought to this country by Bob's great grandmother,*" he wrote underneath his recipe's heading. "*You will find it simple to make, and it will have your guests raving.*"

It all sounds pretty innocent. But anyone who knew Bob Druva also knew there had to be something more mischievous in the oven.

After all, this was the man who went around at Christmastime leaving notes in his neighbors' mailboxes reading, "Congratulations! Out of 20 entries in the neighborhood Christmas decorations contest, you have placed 23rd!" When an attorney across the street held a party, Druva was the one who put up a sign near his yard that read, "Parking: $3; Lawyers, $6."

This was the guy who would buy his mother-in-law racy Christmas presents from Frederick's of Hollywood.

A quiet, unassuming engineer and corporate vice-president who avoided the spotlight, Druva made a life as a committed company man and straight-laced social volunteer. It was all work he thoroughly believed in and enjoyed. It was also the perfect cover for another punch line.

At first, the ingredients in Druva's Famous Stuffing seem harmless enough—three cups of breadcrumbs along with pinches of salt, pepper, and sage. Then there's the strange one: two cups of unpopped popcorn.

"Stuff the bird. Secure each end with thread and needle. Place the bird in a preheated oven.

"It's not necessary to time this operation," he wrote. *"When the ass blows off, serve the bird."*

Robert L. Druva died September 22, 2001, in Pine. He was seventy-nine.

"TWO REMARKABLE THINGS HAPPENED in Pueblo, Colo. in 1921. They had a great flood and I was born," Druva wrote in a three-page autobiography titled "My Life—Until Now."

"They shot off a cannon the day I arrived," he continued. "Some of my critics say, how sad it was they missed."

As he grew up, young Bobby spent much of his time with his grandfather, who immigrated from Germany to help repair and maintain the Arkansas Valley's giant John Deere sugar beet machines. As his grandfather tinkered, Bobby learned every gear and soon knew he wanted to be an engineer.

"I got the football craze in high school, but gave it up after two weeks on the team," he wrote. "I had to retire because of a stomach ailment (no guts)."

It was about the same time he met a girl named Annalee in physics class. Several years later, as rumors of the impending war spread, they decided they didn't want to go to school one day, so they drove down to the Taos courthouse in New Mexico and got married. They kept it secret until he enlisted with the Air Force a few months later, and their parents gave them another wedding, this time in a church.

After serving stateside helping to train pilots during the war, Druva moved to Fort Collins to attend Colorado State University under the GI Bill.

"He was out of the box and could approach things from a different angle. Very down to earth, and not very conventional," said Gordon Johnson, a classmate who remained a lifelong friend. "We had particular projects we had to design (for class). He came up with the idea that he was going to design a brassiere with some steelworks in it," Johnson said. "He came up with quite elaborate designs."

After earning a mechanical engineering degree in 1948, Druva's job hunt didn't last long. While fitting the young graduate for a suit, a tailor told him he should try a new firm called Stearns-Roger, with whom the tailor had several favorite customers. Druva would spend the next thirty-five years there.

"He was very personable, quite easy to get along with, as opposed to some engineers who can be kind of priggish," said Aaron Green, who worked with Druva for nearly three decades at Stearns-

Roger. "He was quiet; he wasn't shy, but he wasn't ebullient. He didn't bubble over and overwhelm you.

"Still, his sense of humor always came through."

Throughout their lives, friends and business associates would periodically receive hand-drawn greeting cards and immediately knew whom to thank (or blame). On one of the cards, he had drawn a statue of a businessman on a pedestal with the words "Now that you're famous you have nothing to worry about." Inside the card he wrote, "except pigeons."

FROM A CARDBOARD BOX found in the attic, the family pulled out dozens of framed certificates that Bob Druva never hung on a wall.

While at Stearns-Roger, he helped organize the company's participation in a program that donated corporate jets to fly doctors to rural towns in Colorado. In his spare time he volunteered to take underprivileged kids to ball games. But most of his time was spent with the family—wife Lee and children Marianne, Mark, and Nancy—which also wasn't immune from his stunts. When he attended parent-teacher meetings, he always seemed to pay rapt attention to the teacher, scribbling on his tablet the whole time. When he came home, he would present his kids with a caricature of the teacher.

In 1987 he retired from the company, rating the experience "a 9.5 out of 10." It gave him plenty of free time for more pranks—such as the time his wife held a formal coffee party at their home.

"When we were leaving after one of these coffees, one of the ladies said, 'Is your husband a commercial artist?'" Lee Druva remembered. "I didn't think anything of it until I was cleaning up and I noticed he had put price tags on all of our paintings, as if they were his."

Despite his financial success, he remained frugal. When white loafers were popular, he painted his black ones with shoe polish instead of buying new ones. When it came to his family, however, money was rarely a consideration.

Throughout his retirement, the couple took their children all over the world on trips. For the Druvas' fiftieth wedding anniversary, he rented an enormous suite at the top of the Broadmoor Hotel and invited the entire clan to celebrate.

In order to satisfy the whole family (grandchildren included) for the anniversary dinner, he bought take-out fried chicken. For the centerpiece, he ordered fifty red roses.

WHENEVER LEE DRUVA had to plan a social event or invite friends over for dinner, Bob would inevitably pipe in with his dinner suggestion.

"Hot dogs and champagne," he would say. "Hot dogs and champagne."

Though the request was rarely granted, he never tired of asking for it—a meal that spanned his life's accomplishments, from his childhood growing up during the Great Depression to a successful career, all of it spiked with smiles.

"After we had the interment of the ashes a week ago, we all came back here to the house," his wife said.

"In his honor, we all had hot dogs and champagne."

The Woman Who Outlived Her Tombstone

Della K. Evans

THE DATE ON THE GRAVESTONE is wrong. It's been wrong for nearly two years.

It's nobody's fault, really. Della Evans ordered the stone after her husband died and figured they might as well put her name on it, too.

Over the next several decades she outlived her siblings, her friends, and both her children.

Nobody thought she would outlive her own headstone.

"EVANS," the rock reads. "James W. 1900–1973. Della K. 1898–19—"

She had always figured she would go first, but when her husband died she had to take care of things. She always could take care of things. At the beginning of her life, she learned the independence she would need at the end of her life; in between she saw three centuries.

On a cold December day inside the cemetery in Brighton, after the last prayers were said, her friends nod at the date below her name on the headstone and can't help but smile.

"How about that," one of them says. "Della would have liked that."

Della K. Evans died December 2, 2001. She was 103.

EIGHTEEN PEOPLE, MOST OF THEM topped with white or gray hair, sit in the tiny church in Hudson.

"One hundred and three years. How can we do her justice in only a few minutes?" asks the Rev. Francis Xavier. "Can we do her justice? No. But here are a few details of her life."

He looks down at his notes.

"1898," he says. "I can't even imagine."

Even at one hundred years old, she remembered her early childhood in Greensburg, Missouri—the smell of her grandmother smoking on a corncob pipe and of clothes made from flour sacks. Her father thought his job as a blacksmith would keep them happy for years but was put out of work by the Industrial Revolution. At the beginning of the twentieth century, he joined the railroad and moved the family to Yuma in eastern Colorado.

When she was fifteen years old, Della traveled back to Missouri by herself, where she earned a teaching certificate from Culver-Stockton College. She returned to Yuma to teach grade school.

In 1925 she married another Yuma railroad man, Jim Evans, in Loveland. They hiked up Berthoud Pass for their honeymoon, but—in a story she loved to tell and he learned to endure—he couldn't figure out how to set up their tents, and their first night together was saved by a troop of passing Boy Scouts.

The Depression was especially rough on her. Both parents died in 1929. Della and Jim hocked the car and managed to scrape together enough money to buy a grocery store on Pearl Street in Denver. In 1940 Jim found another job with the railroad, and they were off again, traveling the area around northeast Colorado and western Nebraska. In 1954 they finally settled down in Hudson, where they made a home inside the railroad depot.

"We always liked it because our parents would put us on the train and it stopped at our grandparents' house," says grandson Jim Evans. "Literally right in front of the house."

A FEW YEARS AGO, SOME FRIENDS took Della Evans to see the film *Titanic*. When it was over, they asked her what she thought.

"Well," she said. "I already knew all that."

When she was ninety-eight, some friends took her to the mall around Christmastime and she said she had never sat on Santa's lap. So she did. She never told anyone what she whispered in his ear.

A sense of playfulness, she said, was the key to longevity.

"She kept making new friends and losing them to old age. But I think it made her stronger," says her grandson. "When you begin to outlive all your friends, some people go one way and some go another. I think it made her stronger, not weaker."

Few things depressed her, but she couldn't help crying when she read stories about small children dying before their time. Why am I still around? she wondered, when little children have to die?

When she started asking those kinds of questions, she headed back to the James Memorial United Methodist Church in Hudson, where she taught Sunday school until she was ninety-one years old, learning with each lesson.

"She said she was glad the Lord hadn't given her everything she'd prayed for," one of her friends says during her funeral service. "Otherwise she said she'd be in a big mess."

When her son, Jim, had a stroke, she took him into her home in Hudson and cared for him until his death in 1994. They buried him in her cemetery plot, next to his father, and chiseled his name on the back of the stone.

Her second son, David, died in 1998, in California. By then she was living with friends in Sheridan, Wyoming. Eventually, she even outlived their care and moved to a nursing home in Sheridan.

During one of his last visits with his grandmother, Jim Evans remembers asking her about her childhood. At the funeral reception inside the church in Hudson, he pulls out a piece of paper he's scribbled on, something he tucked into the front of her scrapbook.

"The last time I saw her she kept repeating this, so I wrote it down," he says, looking down at the paper. "She just kept saying it over and over. I guess it's her philosophy of life."

Life is not a dream
Life is reality
Life is to perceive to pursue
Life is the labor of love.

A Gardener of Words

Preston Arly Coble

AMONG THE FRESH LOAM AND LEAVES in her yard, Barbara Hyde kneels near a patch of pass-along plants.

"This is a tiny little iris that's been in one Longmont family for generations. They gave it to me to keep," she says. "Gardeners do a lot of that. They'll say, 'This has been in my family for generations, please keep it going.' They're pass-along plants."

Among the tiny sprouts that only growers know, she leans over another place—one reserved for the fellow she calls the Grand Old Man of Gardening—and the plants he passed along.

"This is where they are, his poppies," she says to the soil at her home in Littleton. "They are spectacular."

As the pass-along story goes, Preston Coble was driving back from a trip to Alaska when he glimpsed a flash of pink along the side of the road, and the sight stopped him. He gathered a few seeds from the flowers he'd never seen before and brought them back to Colorado, where he shared them with Hyde, the instructor in his Master Gardener class.

"Pretty soon, everybody knew about Pres' poppies," Hyde says. "And every year they have lots of seeds, so we would collect them in a baby food jar and people would come in for Pres' poppies. Now they're scattered all over the place."

At the patch of plants in her front yard, Hyde stands up, still looking down.

"I'll pass on a lot of plants, too," she says. "There are a lot of different things you pass along."

Preston Arly Coble died December 7, 1999. He was ninety-seven.

THE "COLLECTED POEMS OF PRESTON A. COBLE" are printed in simple hand-scrawled letters on orange and brown construction paper, the colors of fall. His words were often about his garden. Few people outside his garden ever saw his poems.

> *If you have an urge for planting*
> *A flower or a tree,*
> *Now is the time to start planning*
> *The kind it's going to be.*
> *Whether for fruit or shade or flower*
> *Or to hide an unsightly view,*
> *There should be one here somewhere*
> *That should be right for you.*
> *And when you plant that tree or flower*
> *And see it thrive and grow*

You will get a certain happy feeling
That some folks may never know.

— from "Time for Planting"

Preston Coble was born June 8, 1902, in a farmhouse at Topaz, Missouri, a wide spot in the road that has long since vanished. The tenth of ten children, he attended a school named after his family; the building has long since burned down. In 1921 he wed Orpha Ann Reed and they stayed married longer than most people stay alive.

In 1927 the couple moved to Longmont, where he took jobs at a few farms before joining on at the Kuner-Empson canning factory. He would stay there for decades. Meanwhile, Ann Coble opened a dress store—she was the social one, always immaculately kempt. He kept to himself, clad in flannel, quietly watching the plants grow and the world change.

"He was a man. People don't know much what that term means anymore," says his son, Gerald. "He didn't say much, but what he did say was to the point. It was pretty much a standard American life for the time. It was a life that was not at all extraordinary, but is typical of those who were born before there was a Ford Motor Company or an airplane, before there was electricity."

All the while, he kept the garden, and his poems. After he retired, they kept him.

The old Coble School
Where I got my start
In reading and writing
But with no real art

Has gone the way
Of all one room schools
And the children now ride
In motor pools
They now ride into town
Twenty miles away
And don't get home
In time to play
In the wooded hills
Which are so close by
Or give the old swimming hole a try
Of course that is progress
Or so the wise ones say
To the one room school
For me far away

— from "Our Old School Is Gone"

Eric and MarySue Rice met the man over the backyard fence, underneath his enormous redbud trees that, like Preston Coble, crossed property lines.

"He's the quintessential ordinary Joe. He wasn't a famous inventor or anything like that," Eric Rice says. "If you're looking for some sort of revelation, he wasn't the guy you're looking for. He was just the guy next door."

The Rices remember Coble—then in his early nineties—coming over every morning to say hello to the couple and their dog. "Yep," the man would drawl as the Labrador slobbered all over him. "I got to come over and get my bath."

"The first thing we noticed about them was that every afternoon he and Ann would just sit on the back porch and just enjoy the afternoon," Eric Rice says. "You know, like life is supposed to be like."

Coble never bragged that he was the state's sixteenth certified Master Gardener, a designation bestowed to him in the mid-1970s by the Colorado State Extension Agency. After graduating from the class, he spent his retirement manning the phones at the agency and at local nurseries, tapping an internal encyclopedia on subjects he never really needed a class to learn.

"If you wanted to know about gardening, he'd talk all day," Eric Rice says. "There were always people coming by. He'd take you around the backyard and show you the trees, the poppies. He was very proud."

For the people willing to make the effort to make it past the garden, to really sit and listen, Coble would keep talking.

"He was proud of his ancestry. He used to talk about the school his father and his uncle built. He used to talk about the Indian in him; he liked to talk about that a lot," Rice says. "Again, nothing special. Just ... the kind of stuff this country was built on."

We have had so much happiness and our share of gloom
But I would not trade it for a trip to the moon
Tho' she gives me hell when I get dirt on the floor
I think I love her just all the more.

—from "There Has Been Some Changes Made"

Orpha Ann died in 1993, leaving Preston alone for the first time in his life, at ninety-one years old. He had recovered from a stroke to care for his wife in her last months but had a more difficult time as the days passed without her. He started chewing tobacco; he forgot to eat. In 1996, his son convinced him to move closer to his great-great grandchildren, and he agreed to make the trek to an assisted care home in Florida.

Eric and MarySue Rice had since moved to a newer house in a trendier part of town. When they heard about Pres' plans, they saw a chance to return to the trees and the stories, and offered to buy the one-hundred-year-old home. Pres agreed to pass it along.

"If anyone was going to understand the sentimental value of this property ... to bring the yard back to some amount of showcase, to understand the legacy and the history," Eric Rice says, it was he and his wife. "It meant a lot to us, and I think it meant a lot to Pres."

Inside the house, the Rices have kept many of the Cobles' furnishings—from the old grandfather clock and treadle sewing machine to Pres' box of hinges in the basement and his wife's collection of ceramic chickens. The year Coble moved to Florida, the Rices entered a couple of his plants at the Boulder County Fair. His old smoke tree, so-called because when you look through the feathery blooms in the right sunlight they look like puffs of smoke, won best of show.

Despite saying that Coble's life probably didn't offer any revelations, as he sits in Preston Coble's old house, Rice has one.

"You know, the more I think about it, maybe that's the problem with modern society," he says. "There aren't enough people content with who they are."

> *Sixty-five years ago today*
> *Is when I first saw the light of day.*
> *My dad was harvesting early wheat*

And came home for a bite to eat.
When told he had an eleven pound boy
His expression probably was not all pure joy.
For that meant ten kids he would have to feed.
Not an easy task for a man, indeed.
But I have often felt sorry for my little mother
For she never expected to have another
For several years and nine kids back
She must have thought she was free from that attack.
Oft times I have wondered if it is best
To have ten kids all in one nest
But I honor my parents and I am very glad
Otherwise I would not be signing letters
From your great-granddad.

— from "June 8, 1967"

In the backyard, the tall redbud trees still stand, among old rosebushes, grapevines, wisteria, and a dwarf California redwood. There's an almond tree along with buckeyes, maples, locusts, gooseberries, elderberries, plums, cedars, and an oak. And there's that old smoke tree.

"Pres had a gardening philosophy that if something had enough gumption to grow somewhere, it's growing there because it wants to, and if it has enough energy to grow there, he wasn't going to be the one to stop it," Rice says.

"It was the same philosophy he had with people."

Though he always voted and read the paper every day, Coble never talked politics. Though he read his Bible every night, he never preached. His conversations were of what grew before him and what was left behind.

"It's fun to listen to Pres. He remembered when an old Civil War vet lived on the corner at the end of the street. He knew the stories of this area before it was a town," Rice says. "This whole hill used to be a giant apple orchard; now there are only three of the trees left. We have one of them in our backyard."

Among the new life and old growth behind his home, Eric Rice walks over to the apple tree and looks up at the buds that will soon bear fruit.

"They're real sweet. They're a real old-fashioned kind," he says. "Something you can't find anymore."

Love Stories
from a Plane Crash

Glenn Davis, Robert Jones, Ryan Sanders

SHE WORRIED ALL THROUGH BREAKFAST, and he knew she did, but that was OK. It was part of the deal.

It had been more than a month since she had found him on the couch and asked him what was wrong. The answer had shocked her, then warmed her. He was thinking of her again.

"I'm thinking I should sell my share of the airplane," he said. She looked at him, baffled.

"You're really afraid of it, you don't enjoy it, and you never will enjoy it," he said. "It costs us a lot of money, and you don't like it."

"That's going to really piss me off if you do that," she said. "You have to fly. It's you. It's a part of you."

She had seen the way he was when he was flying, when he was thinking about flying. He glowed.

She knew she worried too much. His job was, after all, the study of air. She knew she couldn't be the one to keep him out of it.

"Here's the deal," she said. "You have to allow me to worry. The deal is, I get to worry, and you get to fly."

Inside the basement of their home in Boulder, Maria Neary draws her hand over a quilt she made for her husband, Ryan Sanders.

"Fly me to the moon, and let me play among the stars," the quilt reads, among cutout stitches of airplanes. On the back, she printed, *"For Ryan, my very best pal. My inspiration. The love of my life."*

"He was so incredibly passionate about flying. He loved it, but he would have given it up for me," she says.

"I could have stopped him from going Monday morning. I could have flipped out and stood there crying, saying 'I'm really worried' and 'I don't feel good.' I look back on that and I know that if I really lost it he would have said 'I better not do this.'

"But there was no way. There was just no way."

"No," says Laurie Sanders-Cannon, Ryan's sister, as she rubs Neary's back.

"That wouldn't have been in keeping with your deal."

Forty-three-year-old Glenn Davis and fifty-year-old Ryan Sanders had made the trip to San Diego before. This time they would take a more scenic route, over canyon country. Davis planned to attend a conference in California. Sanders wanted to see his nephew's Little League game.

Davis had already bought a commercial plane ticket to San Diego, just in case the weather turned bad, so both of them knew there was no reason to push their luck. They knew the plane. They knew weather. They both knew how to fly and the physics of why.

Davis, a software developer with the University Corporation for Atmospheric Research's Unidata program in Boulder, was instrumental in designing the software program that makes instant weather reports possible over the Internet.

Years before he bought his Mooney M-29 single engine plane, Davis soared as a member of Boulder's Frequent Flyers Productions dance-theater company, which uses low-flying trapezes in its choreography. As part of the group, Davis helped develop the "Aerial Sci-Arts Class," which demonstrates to students the physics of flight.

"He shone so brightly there," says Patti Fay, who performed with him in Frequent Flyers. "He inspired me so deeply in those classes. There's no inspiration like that I saw in those kids' eyes."

THE THIRD PASSENGER in the plane was Robert Jones, but few knew him by that name. Back home in Vernal, Utah, he was Rhonnie. Most everywhere else, friends called him Sage.

For the past several years he traveled across the country as a hobo of sorts, learning what he could from whoever would teach him. The twenty-two-year-old quoted from Chinese and Indian scripture, and even from the movie *Shawshank Redemption*—from which he liked one line in particular: "Either get busy living, or get busy dying."

Everything Jones owned fit into his backpack.

A slight man at five foot four, he was strong, limber, and balanced—able to move from a full handstand to his forearms in one swift move, keeping his legs in the air the entire time. He had been in Boulder for three weeks when he hitched a ride on the plane with Davis after meeting him in a yoga class. Davis had planned to land the plane in Cedar City, Utah, where Jones' girlfriend, Lisa Keays, was just about to graduate from college.

In his pocket, Jones carried her letter:

My beloved Sage, I've been saving this stationery for over a year for special occasions. You're the special occasion, my dear Sage. … I don't know what the future holds, but I do know what I am experiencing right now, and I think of you all the time. My heart races when we talk on the phone. I find myself dreaming of tender kisses and warm embraces. Remember how I told you before you left that I don't want a long distance relationship? Oh, Well.

WHEN THE OPPORTUNITY AROSE for Ryan Sanders to travel to Antarctica, his answer, as usual, made people smile.

Sure he would go, he said. Where else would he have the chance to be the best saxophonist on an entire continent?

At the National Oceanic and Atmospheric Administration in Boulder, Sanders—along with colleague Susan Solomon—made some of the first measurements that would explain the role of chlorofluorocarbons in the depletion of ozone over Antarctica and Greenland. In recognition of his work, he was honored in 1998 with the designation of a piece of Antarctica. A nunatak—an icy ridge on the continent—will forever bear his name.

He would later joke that he and Neary might build themselves a little cabin there some day. Or maybe open a nice bed and breakfast on Sanders Nunatak.

As a child, Sanders gave up Little League to study harder (though he still played for fun and eventually held season tickets to the Colorado Rockies) and was named valedictorian at his high school in California. In band, he was named drum major and continued to study music to the point where he could transcribe songs to sheet music flawlessly.

"I heard his dulcet tones as they echoed out across the snows," Solomon says, recalling their time in Antarctica. "And I know he was the best saxophonist on the continent."

IN SANDERS' BEDROOM, a valentine card still rests on his nightstand. It is one of hundreds.

The tradition began long before the couple was married, when both Neary and Sanders were working at the University of Colorado's Laboratory for Atmospheric and Space Physics. At the time, she had a massive crush on Sanders and created dozens of Valentine's Day cards for the scientist.

"I signed these cards in different handwriting: 'Love from Ramona,' 'Love from Doris,' 'I love you, (signed) Helen.' I sent them to my friends all around the country and would have them fill them out and send them to him, so the valentines would have different postmarks."

One day after the cards began arriving, Sanders and Neary were sitting in a movie theater when he turned to her.

"It's you, isn't it?" he said.

"I couldn't hold it," Neary says. "I couldn't stop laughing."

"That kind of did it. That was the spark."

Each year since, the couple hid Valentine's Day cards for each other around the house. The one on Sanders' nightstand reads simply,

Sweetie, Happy Valentine's Day. XOXOXO.
— M.

Through their fifteen-plus years together, that "crush" never wore off. Frequently, Sanders would read his wife bedtime stories from his collection of Donald Duck and Uncle Scrooge books. Cartoon cels from the animated series hang throughout the house. Near their bathtub sits a flock of rubber duckies.

GROWING UP IN A TINY TOWN in North Carolina, Glenn Davis was, at first glance, an unlikely candidate to become an expert in computers and yoga—a man with a penchant for spontaneous dancing and the low-flying trapeze.

As his friends know, the first glance at Davis was often deceiving.

One day when Glenn was young, his sister Sara Wilson says, their father, Reeves, ordered a bottle of alcohol to be brought to the house. Reeves had already lost his driver's license, and another bottle meant a bad night was likely for the family.

As soon as the bottle arrived, she says, Glenn grabbed it and ran out the door. He didn't come home for days to avoid the inevitable retribution.

Glenn "was our protector," along with their mother, Wilson says. "And he fought for the good."

FOUR TIMES A WEEK, Neary wakes up early and heads straight for the gym. On May 3, 1999, she stayed in.

The night before, she and Sanders had sat down for another long candlelit dinner, where they talked and laughed. Sometimes they would just watch the wax drip.

"He was slouching in the chair, and I gave him a hard time about slouching," she says. "He asked for a head rub so he came over here and I rubbed him for about an hour."

That morning, she had breakfast with her husband.

"You'll call me when you get to Cedar City, right?" she made him promise, even though he always called.

"OK, I promise," he said. "I'll call."

She worried, and he knew she did, but neither said anything. That was the deal. Instead, as the truck pulled away, they waved— full-arm, floppy-handed waves—like two little kids.

ON THE AFTERNOON OF MAY 3, Davis radioed the control tower at the Cedar City airport that he intended to land, despite a raging thunderstorm, because he was running low on fuel and the plane was beginning to ice up.

The storm threw massive balls of hail at the plane, which disappeared from radar shortly before 3 p.m. An hour later, an army Blackhawk helicopter found the wreckage five miles from the airport. There were no survivors.

RYAN SANDERS' YOUNG FRIEND, Willy Douglas, keeps a book called "Questions for Ryan."

"Ryan was the kind of guy who knew the answers to questions nobody else did," Neary says. "He would seem to have an answer on every level. Why is the sky blue? Why is the ocean different colors in different places? Who played Wally on 'Leave it to Beaver'?"

"I told him to keep that book up," Sanders-Cannon says. "You can learn a lot by continuing to ask questions.

"Sometimes you can learn more from questions than from answers."

After several desperate calls throughout the afternoon, Lisa Keays found out from the television news that a single engine plane headed from Colorado had crashed. She called the police to confirm what she dreaded, then made plans to visit the crash site.

After years of rebelling against everything Utah had to offer—at times wearing a massive nose ring, fishnet stockings, and makeup, and causing trouble—Rhonnie Jones took the name Sage four years ago, when he began studying yoga.

"Sage means 'a man of wisdom,'" says his mother, Rhondale Jones. "He felt that through all his mistakes in life, he had learned great lessons."

In April, Jones attended his sister's wedding in Utah. After a week together, he and his family were closer than they had been in years.

When Keays arrived at the site of the crash, the plane had just been pulled off the hillside.

"When they pulled the plane out, they ripped up all the sagebrush," she says. "So the whole field smelled like sage."

Inside his pack, Jones always carried a velvet pouch of his most important belongings—a collection that included a small vial of peppermint oil, of which he would place a few drops on his tongue before he kissed her, Keays says.

"In the crash, the vial of peppermint oil broke," she says. "So everything smells like him."

When Patti Fay remembers Glenn Davis off the trapeze, she remembers the time she needed some help setting up her computer, and she knew exactly where to turn.

Once Davis had the computer running, he asked her what she wanted for her "saying."

"What saying?" she asked. "Why do you need a saying?"

"It's what comes on every time you turn on your computer," he said.

"Well," she said, "Why don't you put one in for me."

When she turned on her computer, it flashed the following message:

"Living well is the best revenge."

AT THE NATIONAL CENTER for Atmospheric Research in Boulder, fog often settles in during a storm, shrouding the Boulder landmark in mist. For Glenn Davis' memorial service, there is no view from the windows. The clouds have come all the way down.

As she stands, silhouetted against the gray, Sara Wilson again remembers her brother.

"In our family, the four siblings were the balance," she says. "Glenn was the wind, I was the earth, Jonelle was the fire, and Jamie was the water.

"We're going to carry on that wind."

Before leading the crowd in a traditional New Orleans–style jazz funeral parade around the room, Nancy Smith, artistic director of Frequent Flyers Productions, reads an excerpt from one of Davis' writings that he used to prepare himself for his dances.

My daddy's folks lived in the mountains of western North Carolina, he wrote.

I can remember singing with Mammaw at church. Montmorenci Methodist Church is on a little knoll up above South Hominy

Crick. It's in a big clearing, right on top, at the end of a long, steep driveway.

Mammaw and Pappaw are buried there. Maybe it is a little closer to heaven.

After the crash, Glenn Davis was buried nearby.

MARIA NEARY REACHES UP and touches her shoulders.

"I've been doing this motion a lot," she says. "I can still feel him holding on. Feeling that connection with him."

In front of her are the photos of their fifteen years together. Some of the albums still have room.

"We were life partners," she says. "We were going to grow old together in this house. We used to joke that we live so close to the hospital, we would be able to hobble down 11th Street and visit each other. We were in it for the long haul together.

"Now I'm going to grow old without him."

She grasps the large pewter heart-shaped locket that hangs around her neck.

"Three years ago I entered a contest at an art gallery in Cherry Creek and I won this gift certificate and I bought myself a locket," she says. "I've always wanted a locket. Since I was a little kid I wanted a locket. So I put his picture in it, and I've worn it every day. I've worn it every day for the past three years.

"It's not because Ryan died that I'm going to wear it forever. I've always worn it. He's always been right there."

She cracks open the heart, and peers inside.

"That's him, just grinning," she says, gazing at the tiny photo. "I love that I can see his eyes."

A Century of Life
for a Lost Heartbeat

George Curry Evans

GEORGE EVANS' LIFE BEGAN ALONGSIDE his twin brother, inside a padded shoebox.

"It was the only way (his parents) knew to keep them warm," said Evans' daughter, Judith Cochran. "They were so small."

It was 1901 in New York, and chances for premature babies were slim. When the babies contracted pneumonia at two months old, those chances ran out for one. George's brother, Walter, couldn't outlive his tiny cardboard crib.

For the rest of his life George Evans never forgot the twin brother he never knew—even as the family deteriorated, even as he was sent to orphanages and beaten, even as he ran away, again and again, living alone on the road. He thought of his lost family while staring at the sea during World War I and as he struggled through the Great Depression.

Eventually, Evans would go on to raise a new family the way he had learned rather than the way he had lived. He would help save his sister's life, and his new family would care for him until the end. Through it all, he tried to remember the heartbeat in the shoebox.

"George always said 'I have to live at least until one hundred,' " his daughter said. "He said, 'I have to live once for me, and once for Walter.' "

George Curry Evans died in his sleep June 18, 2001, at his daughter's home in Highlands Ranch. It was the day after Father's Day. He was 100.

IN THE SUMMER OF 2000, George Evans sat in his mobile home in Littleton, where the ninety-nine-year-old cracked open a book of black and white photos he once tried to forget. As a newspaper reporter listened, he forced himself to remember.

"My folks separated when I was a small boy, and my mother put me in four different orphan homes and they all beat me. It was one hell of an early life," he said. "When my father came to get my sister from the orphanage they made him take me too, because they couldn't handle me anymore. I had gotten too mean. I was fighting the world."

George ran away from home, away from the orphanages, and even spent time hiding on an Indian reservation. When he heard there was going to be a world war, he figured that was for him; he was already fighting the world. The seventeen-year-old lied about his age and joined the Navy.

At sea, underneath the billowing smokestacks of the battleship USS *New Hampshire,* Evans spent blinding hours staring at the waves, watching for German submarines.

"I'm a very fortunate person. A very fortunate person. My only contribution to the war was that I ate a lot of beans and saw a lot of saltwater," he said. "I didn't perform any heroic thing. But I'm still alive." Not everyone on his ship could say the same.

"They had the big flu epidemic. In the morning they'd go around and check the hammocks to see how many were dead. They'd come by, pick 'em up, and dump 'em over. If someone was missing, we knew then what had happened," said Evans, who had barely survived smallpox in 1915.

"It was quite a deal," he said. "Quite a deal."

When he returned home, Evans joined a motorcycle daredevil team but quickly realized he wouldn't be around for much longer if he didn't slow down. He began educating himself, swallowing books, and studying through correspondence courses.

"I adopted a plan where I did a lot of reading, and when I came to a word I didn't know, I'd put it on a three-by-five index card," he said. "I figured if I didn't know how to pronounce the word, spell the word, and give a definition, then I didn't know the word. So at one time I had over three thousand words in this collection."

He made it through three years of law school in San Francisco before the money ran out during the Depression. He started over, finding odd jobs in retail shops and eventually ran a wholesale liquor business.

His life up to that point paled with what was about to come next. In 1936 he met Helen Bettencourt.

"This was a marriage made in heaven. I tell you to this day I can't talk about her without ... displaying my emotions," Evans said, his eyes flooding. "We were married for sixty-two years. She was the most wonderful person I ever knew. She had a rough young life, too. She lost her mother when she was seven and her father when she was nine.

"I tell ya. One thing we worked out when we married was that neither one of us was a nothing."

As he reached the end of his photo album, the ninety-nine-year-old continued to reflect.

"I guess you could say I'm a self-made man," he said, closing the cover. "I would see people and I would adopt traits of theirs that I liked. That's how I became a halfway civilized human."

In September of 2000 he moved in with his daughter in Highlands Ranch. George and Helen had moved from California to Colorado in 1992 to be closer to their daughter and grandkids. Before Helen's death in 1998, they extended the family.

"Every veteran (he met) was touched by this man's love, his humor, and his honesty," said Bud Goodwin, commander of Littleton American Legion Post 103, where Evans was an active member.

"To me, George was like my second father," said Goodwin, who served in the Navy during World War II. "He extended my father's presence for me."

George Evans outlived everyone from his childhood. Despite his disagreements with his parents, he buried them both. Throughout his life, he kept in close contact with his two sisters. When one of them almost died decades ago, he gave her a risky, lifesaving blood transfusion. She later said she could feel his blood tingling inside. She died at age ninety-eight.

Though he enjoyed celebrating his birthday, he was usually sad the day afterward, but not because he was another year older. His twin brother was born the day after George. He was sad because it was Walter's birthday.

When asked the inevitable questions about the secret to longevity, Evans would mention his affinity for golf—he shot in the eighties when he was in his nineties—and his insistence on eating ice cream every night. Then there was The Game.

"Baseball, I tell you. The one thing that's kept me active is baseball. I became a Giants fan in the summer of 1912. I was eleven years old," he said. "When you get my age, you tend to sit back and vegetate and go to pot. But I have just as much an interest in baseball today as I did when I was eleven."

He followed the Giants from their days in New York to their time in San Francisco and in between memorized thousands of statistics. He watched Babe Ruth, Willie Mays, and Ted Williams from the bleachers. He would pick up almanacs from years past, reliving his own history. Even during his last few years he was known to watch a baseball game on television while keeping track of another on the radio.

The day before he died, Evans watched the last baseball game of his life on television. The Giants won.

The year before he died, as Evans finished one of his final newspaper interviews, he looked around his daughter's home and thought back to the one he never had as a child.

"There's nothing like a home life," he said. "Nothing can replace it."

There in the living room, the ninety-nine-year-old stood up and extended his hand. He held the handshake tight, until he finished the way he wanted.

"You know the most important word in every language on earth? One word: love," he said. "If we have love, then we can do most anything. I've preached that and I will preach it. Love."

A Treehouse Above It All

Douglas Patrick Donnelly

ATOP HIS SPRAWLING TREEHOUSE among a dozen cottonwoods, the man with the blurry face looked through thick glasses and watched the world through the leaves.

On his perch twenty feet above the ground, Doug Donnelly stood on warped wood that nobody had wanted. The middle-aged man climbed on legs that doctors told him would never work. He designed the treehouse with a mind that was once called useless.

For those people willing to venture up into the trees, Donnelly held out his hand and gave a low chuckle. He then pointed to the ladders that led into his branches and showed visitors where to hold on.

"Our lives—and his world—were totally different," said his sister, Colleen Donnelly Dean. "But thank God for his world. It's an amazing place."

Douglas Patrick Donnelly died January 17, 2004, in Monte Vista, following a heart attack in his sleep, his family said. He was forty-one.

WHEN HE WAS BORN, the infant's face looked out of focus, his eyes crossed, and his features seemed smoothed away. Doctors would later say he had some characteristics of Down's syndrome, but their initial diagnosis said only that "he would be severely mentally retarded" and suggested the best home was an institution. According to his mother, that was never an option.

"We weren't sure what kind of life he was going to have," said Phyllis Donnelly. "It wasn't long before we knew it was going to be a good one."

Due to nerve damage, young Doug couldn't really smile, she said, but anyone could tell when he was trying, because he twitched from cheeks to forehead.

"His smile," his mother said, "was all over his face."

Despite the doctors' initial observations, the family soon realized that the little boy was far more intelligent than most people thought. He attended public schools, taking a combination of special education and regular classes.

Along with school came inevitable teasing, but he found defenders in close friends from his tight, rural neighborhood east of Boulder. Eventually, he figured out how to fight back on his own.

"Even if you did tease him, it wasn't long before he would be your friend," said Chris Clyncke, a longtime neighbor and lifelong pal. "If you laughed at him, he'd just laugh back at you. Because he knew better. And then he was teasing you. It was amazing—you'd think you were getting Doug, and instead Doug would get you."

It wasn't long before he was among the most popular kids in school. In eighth grade, he was elected class president of Nevin Platt Junior High, after promising to bring more junk food into the lunchroom. (Once administrators told him his platform was impossible to implement, he respectfully resigned.)

Then in 1982, he accomplished another goal that some said was unattainable: He walked across the stage at Boulder High School, diploma in hand. When he turned around, he was met with a standing ovation.

AFTER GRADUATION, DONNELLY took a job on an assembly line at a company that made medical devices. When that company moved overseas, he took a similar job elsewhere and worked full time until recently.

Still, few friends or co-workers knew of the problems they couldn't see: a malformed spine that resulted in back problems, throbbing in his legs, and other periodic medical struggles.

The face that wouldn't allow him to smile properly, his mother said, also kept him from crying.

"He was in pain every day of his life," Phyllis Donnelly said. "But very few people knew it."

Donnelly began each day before the sun, in front of the newspaper, then stacks of magazines—especially *Scientific American* and *Discover*—poring over each article, circling key phrases, rearranging words and sentences, responding to articles in his own block letters.

"Who was the first Hominid?" posed a headline in a recent issue of *Discover*.

"My ex-boss was the first subhuman," Doug replied in the margin.

"Why do we walk upright?" another headline asked.

"To get a better view," he wrote.

He often spoke in silly antonyms constructed to make people giggle, delivered in his deadpan, Eeyore-like drone: Safeway was "Dangerous path." City Market was "Town Market," and Wal-Mart was "Mal-Wart."

"He makes you pause and stop to appreciate those things that you never see," said Brian Cabral, assistant head coach of football at the University of Colorado, who lived with the Donnellys while attending CU and shared the basement with Doug.

"So many little things," Cabral said. "Simple things."

WHEN HIS FAMILY MOVED TO MONTE VISTA in 2002, it wasn't long before Donnelly saw the forest, the trees, and the opportunity.

Soon he was hitching rides on trucks to the lumber store, asking if they had any wood they didn't need. With the help of his extended family, he quickly built a place of his own, where he read his magazines and science fiction books, watched the world, and fell asleep to the rush of the nearby Rio Grande.

At his funeral in Boulder, his nephew Tyler Dean read from one of his uncle's most prized possessions, a book titled, *Treehouses, the Art and Craft of Living out on a Limb.*

Inside a church packed with nearly three hundred mourners, Dean read a poem from a well-worn copy of the book—one that had spent hours with Doug Donnelly, up in the branches:

TREEHOUSES

They inspire dreams
They represent freedom
from adults or adulthood
from duties and responsibilities
from an earthbound perspective.
If we can't fly with the birds
at least we can nest with them.

The Barflies Say Goodbye

Patricia J. Wagster

THROUGH THE WISPY CIGARETTE SMOKE and low roar of both laughter and sobbing, the barflies raise their glasses inside Northglenn Moose Lodge No. 2166.

"She was a hard knocks lady, but she was something," says Dottie McCarty, as she settles into her seat at the old wooden bar.

"She was one of a kind," says Kathy Etheridge.

"To Pat," she says, and they raise their drinks.

Above them, dozens of giant plastic flies hang from the bar. The women smile.

"Pat will always be looking over us," McCarty says.

At the front of the bar hangs a glowing Michelob sign, the kind usually reserved for scribbling drink specials.

"Our Dear Pat passed away this morning at 9:23," the sign reads. *"Memorial will be here."*

Patricia J. Wagster died January 31, 1999. She was fifty.

"Hard life," says daughter Dawn Zielinski as she stands at the door of the lodge. "She worked hard, she played hard, and paid hard."

Emerging from the haze into the parking lot, the woman takes a deep breath.

"Mom was born in Illinois, she started at Catholic schools, going to church, and she was a rebel from then on out. That's how she lived her life. Tattoos, Harleys. She was pregnant at fourteen, and her grandparents gave up her daughter for adoption. We're still trying to find her (daughter), to tell her."

In 1972, the family moved to Denver, where Pat Wagster would spend the next twenty years raising four children by herself. She worked mostly as a bartender, once as a meat packer, but mostly as a bartender.

"We lived in a trailer park, nothing fancy, and the last six years she spent working here at the Moose," Zielinski says. "Tough lady."

As she walks back inside and stands by the giant moose head on the wall, Zielinski looks into the crowd. When her mother got sick a couple years ago, it was the people at the lodge that raised money to pay many of the bills. Someone in the bar anonymously paid the rent on her trailer for the past year. This was the place where she had her last birthday party.

"This is her extended family. This is where she found comfort, this is where she found security, this is where she found total, uncontrolled commitment," her daughter says. "People loved her for who she was, and that was the first time in her life she found something like that."

AT A TABLE TO THE SIDE of the bar, a man nicknamed Stub sits near a woman nicknamed Bubba. "Stub" Foley runs the Moose Lodge. "Bubba" Gresham is the secretary.

"She had a way about her that made everyone like her," Stub says.

"She always thought a lot of you," Bubba says.

"I thought a lot of her," Stub says.

"She called me up one day and told me she'd need a little time off, because they told her she had cancer," Stub says. "That was a bad, bad day for us. She fought that all the way through. She fought real hard; she wouldn't give up."

"Pat wasn't one to give up," Bubba says.

They look over to the bar, where the Wagster daughters are hugging people.

"She raised those kids by herself. That's not an easy life," Stub says.

"No, that wouldn't be an easy life," says Kitty Foley, Stub's wife, who sits nearby.

Rumor around the bar said it was the Foleys who paid the lot rent on Pat's trailer. When the question comes up, they avoid it.

"The place just took care of her," Stub says. "When she got in trouble, we came together to help her."

WAGSTER WAS DIAGNOSED with breast cancer at forty-nine. For the next eighteen months she endured six chemotherapy treatments, two radiation treatments, and two experimental therapies.

"She continued to want to work; she didn't want to give up her job," Zielinski says. "So my sister Lisa and I switched off working here on her shifts."

The daughters donated all their wages to help out their mom. Every Thursday, the tip jar was emptied and every penny went to help pay Wagster's bills. She continued to attend the Women of the Moose meetings, making presents for children. Often, she returned the favors in humor.

On Halloween, since her head was shaved, she came as a clown. She was known to wear a wig to cover her head and was also known to throw the wig at smart alecks at the bar.

"After she had a radical mastectomy, people would ask how her breast was doing and she'd flip (her prosthetic breast) out of her shirt, hand it over and say, 'it's fine, just fine,'" Zielinski says, smiling, shaking her head.

To raise more money, the lodge began selling giant plastic flies for $5; anyone who bought a fly could write their name on it and hang it above the bar. They raised thousands of dollars.

"Pat had her name on one of those flies right from the beginning, so I guess she was an old barfly herself," says Butch Morehart, who was there for Wagster's first day at the lodge. "She came here as a bartender, and she found a home. She found a home is what she did."

AT THE TABLE IN THE BACK, Bubba lowers her head.

"She'd probably slap every one of us for crying," she says. "She didn't want anyone feeling sorry for her."

"She could be a hardball when it came to compassion," Stub says.

"One time things were going real well, so we got all three of the bartenders roses," he says. "We put hers behind the bar, and then she came in and found them and asked 'What the hell are these doing here?' We said, 'Those are for you, we got those for you.'

"Boy, she cried like a baby. She didn't want anyone to see her crying, but she couldn't help it," Bubba says.

"No place'd ever done that for her, I suppose."

Lullabies for Lions, Bears, and Baby Warthogs

Dennis A. Roling

FROM THE CAGE COMES A LOW, strong rumble—the animal kingdom's most powerful purr.

"You hear that noise she's making?" asks Marlene Kumpf, feline keeper at the Denver Zoo, as she listens to the lioness. "She made that sound a lot for Denny. She used to love it when Denny came in here. She used to love hearing his voice. When he was here she would stand here and wait to be rubbed. She made that sound a lot."

Denny Roling knew where to scratch the lions in the den and how to soothe the baby monkeys in the nursery. He stayed up all night with infant polar bears in his home and watched in awe at elephants he saw on an African safari. He saw the animals everywhere. He saw them in his dreams.

"He had one dream where he was back in Africa," Kumpf says. "In the dream, he said it was dark and he could hear the lions roaring but he couldn't see them. The lions were roaring so loud. They roared so loud that they woke him up."

As she walks through the feline house, Kumpf points to the place where the snow leopard would play peek-a-boo with Roling. She remembers that during the blizzard of 1982, he was one of the first staffers to make it through the snow.

She recalls the man who made lions purr and the people he touched along with the animals. Then she remembers a dream of her own.

"On Sunday night, I had a dream that many of the cats I take care of had escaped into the parking lot. This should have been a serious situation, but at the same time it seemed OK. The lions were happy. ... Our lioness Lucy was roaring and roaring in the parking lot, and it got so loud that I woke up.

"Then I realized it was Denny. He let me know."

Dennis A. Roling died March 20, 2000, after a seventy-eight-day battle with myelody splasia, a rare form of leukemia. He was forty-seven.

IN THE VIEWING AREA of the zoo nursery, a baby monkey peers out from a keeper's lap at cooing visitors. On the other side of the glass, the nursery is quieter than usual.

"One day Denny was singing to the animals and he didn't realize his (walkie-talkie) was left on, so he was broadcasting to the entire zoo," says Cindy Bickel, a veterinary technician. "The keepers had wondered what was going on, if someone had left the radio on, but it was Denny, singing to the animals."

In his twenty-two years at the zoo, Roling's songs served as lullabies for the nursery's miniature menagerie. Some animals heard the hymns Roling learned in church, some were soothed by the classics he learned as part of the Denver Gay Men's Chorus. He knew the ones that liked "Danny Boy" and the bobcat that hissed at him when he sang the tune (Roling used the open-mouthed hissing as a chance to pop a bottle of formula into the bobcat's mouth).

Bickel says she'll never forget Denny Roling's singing voice. She heard it during the day, to quiet the cubs. She heard it at 3 a.m., when the monkeys started screaming.

"People just see the fun stuff, the cuddly stuff, and the little baby animals," she says. "They don't see the work, the effort, that went into getting the babies that far."

She walks into the "hoof ward," where Roling would often curl up with baby antelope and reindeer in the straw. Together, the keepers stayed up late with the famous polar bear cubs Klondike and Snow, who were abandoned by their mother in 1994. They also watched over the not-so-famous, such as the litter of warthogs that required constant care.

Just outside the nursery, Bickel looks out at a makeshift play yard for the baby animals. At Roling's funeral service the day before, she had played a videotape of Roling running around with Kwanza the rhino, TJ the tiger, and Bungee the spider monkey.

"Over there in the bushes, that's where we'd play with TJ. Around here is where he ran with Kwanza. This is the tree where ..." her voice trails off into tears. She points and begins again.

"Denny would get up in that tree with the babies, with the red pandas, with Bungeeman. And they would climb that tree."

She stands for a full minute, silently looking at the empty yard.

"I'll always remember him in the tree."

BEHIND THE NURSERY IS A PLACE often overlooked during stories of cute zoo babies. It was a place Denny Roling couldn't ignore.

"Over time I've gotten sensitive about going in there," Bickel says of the zoo's necropsy room, where dead animals are examined. "That can be really hard, but Denny did it. He was a strong person, not just physically but mentally. It was nice to have his shoulder to cry on."

When Roling was a child, growing up on the banks of the Mississippi River in Clinton, Iowa, he would hold funeral services for the neighborhood pets, burying them in his mother's Avon cosmetics boxes. As an adult, only the animals changed.

"When my two rhinos died, he knew how much I loved those rhinos and how much they meant to me," says Chris Bobko, a rhino keeper at the zoo. "He personally made sure that I had some of the ashes from each rhino, in separate urns, to take back to Africa. That touched me so deeply. He knew the pain, and he helped ease that transition. It's one of my most cherished memories of him."

When an animal died at the zoo, whether from old age or illness, Roling often handled the cremation. Just as he had when he was a child, Roling made a point to hold a private memorial service for each one.

For docent Linda Cayton, the animal funerals were an extension of Roling's sense of giving that spanned species.

"I really respected how he understood the fatality of life," Cayton says. "The amount of time he took with some of those babies, he just bonded with them. But not all of them make it."

For the ones that didn't make it, Roling had a simple philosophy, one that his friends now find themselves repeating without him.

"He just said, 'Well, they had to go back. They weren't ready yet. They had to go back.'"

BRUCE JOBE KEEPS A POSTCARD that Roling sent him from a zoo-sponsored safari in Africa. On the front is a picture of an elephant. On the back, Roling wrote, *"I wish you could hear what I've heard, and see what I've seen."*

"He just absorbed everything," Jobe says. "He experienced everything he came in contact with."

As he tries to understand Roling's death, Jobe has his own simple philosophy.

"It was just like he was on loan to us. He was just on loan."

In the twelve years they lived together, Roling and Jobe hosted monkeys, warthogs, and kangaroos, along with the city's most popular polar bear cubs.

"It was kind of normal for the neighborhood to see that we're bringing a baby reindeer out of the Honda and into the house," Jobe says. "I remember an antelope named Tracy. One Christmas she would just go over and lay underneath the Christmas tree and peek out from underneath the branches. Our lives were so filled."

In the time he spent away from the animals, Roling devoured hobbies while looking for ways to share them. He took classes in photography, glass blowing, jewelry making, stained glass, sculpting, and upholstery. He volunteered at the Denver Museum of Nature and Science and with hospital patients infected with HIV. Like his time, he gave away most of his crafts.

"Denny was also a storyteller," Jobe says, noting that Roling never missed a performance by African storyteller Opalanga Pugh. Of all the performances they saw, all the stories they heard, Jobe remembers one in particular: a time when the storyteller began her talk by asking everyone to think of a positive aspect of their personality.

"I'll never forget it," Jobe says. "Denny turned and said, 'Appreciate. I try to appreciate everything in my life. Everything that comes before me and through me.

"Appreciate.'"

A Home for All
that Disappears

Eleanor C. Foley

CONDOMINIUMS SPROUT INTO A VAST beige horizon along the busy winding road, but those who know where to look can find a small patch of alfalfa just off the blacktop.

The tallgrass still grows above the place where the cars whiz past, just below the canal that old timers call "the ditch," leading to daffodils, hollyhocks, and a little house with a horseshoe over the front door.

"*Welcome to our farm,*" reads the hand-painted sign inside Eleanor Foley's modest white home in southeast Denver. Inside on the kitchen table rests the story of her life: "50 years on the High Line Canal: A Colorado Memoir of Houses, Horses and Land."

We held our breath each morning as the land unrolled beneath us, stretching to meet the inverted bowl of sky, she wrote. *Far beyond the sprawling city below, we beheld Pikes Peak to the south, Mt.*

*Evans to the west and Longs Peak to the north. On clear days we
viewed the white mountaintops of Wyoming. For years animal life,
ball cacti and wildflowers outnumbered humans along the ditch.*

The pages chronicle times often forgotten.

The manuscript was never published.

*A dirt road became a blacktop street, and still later
condominiums mushroomed all around us,* she continued. *Open
fields were no longer the domain of jackrabbits, foxes and ring-
necked pheasants. Now that the city has crept to our front door, we
are surrounded by townhouses housing folks we'll never learn to
know.*

During her five decades in the little home, Eleanor Foley
witnessed changes in the landscape and helped create changes
for women searching for better lives. She saw the world from
boardrooms and horseback but always returned to the little home
below the big ditch.

"Together in this place," she wrote of her house, *"(my
husband) and I planned our final legacy."*

Eleanor C. Foley died July 6, 2000. She was eighty-six.

THE MEMOIR BEGINS at a service station in Philadelphia, with a
young couple listening to the December 7, 1941, radio broadcast
that froze so many lives. The two had been on their way to look for
a home on the East Coast when they heard President Roosevelt's
voice from the gas station speaker. Bill Foley headed for the Navy,
and the newlyweds decided to meet up in Denver after the war.

Eleanor arrived in Colorado alone, behind the wheel of a 1936
Ford Phaeton, a lightweight open touring car she piloted all the way
from Pennsylvania.

Packed tightly under the back seat canvas were most of my worldly possessions, she wrote. *I had experienced eastern tornadoes, but this was unfamiliar territory and I was uneasy about the strong winds and the billowing black clouds in this western sky. I had visions of being swept into the air like a toy kite and deposited God-knows-where.*

It was far from the first time she was left alone. Though she talked only briefly to friends of her Montana upbringing, she told of a terrible childhood and virtual abandonment by her parents before she found relatives on the East Coast. Despite the rough times, she always spoke of returning to the Rocky Mountains.

After braving the western skies to arrive in Denver, she found a job at the International Trust Company, where her husband would also work after the war. As she moved to other firms, it wasn't long before she became frustrated at the limits imposed on women in business. Unlike most, she set out to change the rules.

"I realized a woman wasn't worth more than $150 a month no matter what she was doing," she wrote.

In 1955 she started her own company, Aurora Business Escrow Service, and was named president of the emerging Aurora chapter of Business and Professional Women.

Meanwhile, the couple had built their dream house in the country on Lower Parker Road (now South Quebec Way), where signals of their friendships could be seen for miles.

Our hillside house, situated on what was then open country, was visible from Colorado Boulevard, she wrote. *When (visitors) left our place, their headlight beams made polka dot ribbons in the falling snow. Red taillights faded gently into the night and disappeared (and) about three miles from the house they came back*

into view. They flashed their automobile lights and we "answered"
by flashing the floodlights. It was our goodnight to one another.

THE DAY AFTER ELEANOR FOLEY'S memorial service, four women
sit around her kitchen table, thumbing through books of photos
and newspaper clippings that their friend was too modest to share.

"There was just something about Eleanor that commanded
a natural respect. A natural respect," says Erwin Buck, who met
Foley through Business and Professional Women.

"She's the grandmother I picked," says Teri Lunsford, who
arrived at the house fifteen years ago to help with the yard and
stayed to help care for Foley. "She was a mentor. She taught by
example."

They talk about how feisty she was, "a pistol" they say,
keeping her independence even after her husband died in 1988. As
Foley aged and slowed, neighbors would watch from their homes
as she shuffled out to the barn to feed the horses. She joined the
Widowed Person's Service group and was quickly elected president,
and continued to fight for the land as a member of the High Line
Canal Preservation Committee.

A tiny office within her home holds the few signs of
her accomplishments. On the wall hang plaques from horse
organizations, governmental agencies, and chambers of commerce—all emblazoned with her name.

"There are only a few that she would let me hang up,"
Lunsford says. "But as I go through her things I keep finding more
and more."

THE FIRST ENTRY IN THE GUESTBOOK for the little white house came from Mabelle and William Hall, in 1948:

May this abode ever be a place of love and good fellowship,
Let it be the inspiration and the source of a very full and happy life to those who dwell herein,
God bless all who come here and tarry within these walls.

Thanks to one of her last gestures, the dedication will prove true long after Eleanor Foley's death.

During the 1980s, Foley was helping care for a 106-year-old friend when she realized that in the race for personal gain, society had forgotten to find a place for the people who helped build it. By then, Foley knew the value of watching over elders—she had helped care for her mother-in-law, who lived with them until the day she died in Foley's arms.

"We saw a need for seniors on limited income, unable to live alone, but not necessarily in need of nursing care," she wrote.

To help find solutions, she and her husband deeded their property to Senior Homes of Colorado. The organization has since built Skyview Village, a senior care home rising from the bottom of her land.

"She could have sold this property for millions," says friend Catherine Lazers Bauer, who helped Foley write her memoir. "But she said, 'This is the only way I can see things.'"

The Foleys also donated a piece of land to the condos across the street, a place known as Foley Park. A sign with their name used to hang in the park but has since disappeared. Eleanor Foley didn't report the sign missing or ask for a new one. In the past few years, she was just happy to lead her horse Chancy down to what was left of the field, to graze in the alfalfa.

Tomorrow there will be a larger family housed on this piece of ground, she wrote. *May it be "home" not alone to humans, but also to the birds, wildflowers, animals and cottonwood trees that have every right to thrive along the High Line Canal. The landscape was there before we were. Yet all things in all time leave hieroglyphics on the land. We hope ours will read well.*

The Life of the Carousel

Robert E. McClelland

THE AFTERNOON OCTOBER SUN SPILLS into the glass eyes of the lion on the eastern plains, his face frozen in the same roar for the past ninety-five years.

"When you're on the lion you're ahead; you're not behind anyone," says Wanda McClelland. "That's what Bob always said. 'The lion is the lead animal.'"

Inside the Kit Carson County Carousel, the king of the beasts leads a gleaming hand-carved herd. In the sun they shine, polished by the hands of thousands of children and the efforts of an entire county. They shine the way Bob McClelland knew they could.

"When they first asked him to do this, he didn't know what he was getting into," his wife says. "He was just a farmer."

When he first saw the carousel, the lead animal was covered in several coats of dull brown varnish, as was the rest of the menagerie. The zebras had no recognizable stripes; the giraffes had no spots. The band organ was in pieces that once housed rats. The background oil paintings were hidden by layers of muck.

"He just had a vision that it would be original," his son John says.

For the past quarter century, Bob McClelland was the keeper of the carousel, the one with the key to the animals. As they started to shine, he found the stories underneath the paint.

"There's the tiger, and if you'll notice the tiger has a touch of blood on his front teeth," says Danyel Brenner, director of Old Town Burlington, who has been working at the carousel since high school.

"He would say that the tiger came up and bit the hindquarter of the Indian pony," she says, "and that's why that hole was (on the pony)."

The kids knew that he always needed to lock the carousel up tight at night, so none of the animals escaped. When they climbed aboard a horse, they had to watch their backs, because a certain old man on the horse behind them kept saying he was going to catch up to them, that he was going to win the race.

As she stands near the old crank that sets things in motion, Brenner remembers Bob McClelland's voice.

"Let's go for a ride. That's what he would always say," she says. "Let's go for a ride."

Robert E. McClelland died June 27, 2000, in Burlington. He was seventy-nine.

BOB MCCLELLAND WAS BORN a few dozen miles away from Burlington, in Kansas, eight years before Kit Carson County bought the old carousel from Elitch Gardens amusement park. At the time, Elitch's wanted to upgrade to a model where the animals moved up and down. The folks in Burlington figured the stationary creatures were just fine; the kids there knew how to use their imaginations.

As young Bob and his family struggled through the Great Depression on their family farm, so did the people in nearby Colorado. Some homeless families found shelter inside the carousel, which was soon shut down. By then the county commissioners had lost their jobs for such a "frivolous" purchase.

In 1946, Bob moved across the border to Colorado and began leasing a 692-acre tract of grassland by the Smoky Hill River. He soon transformed the land into wheat fields.

"They said he was outstanding in his field," his son says. "Whenever anyone asked where he was, that was also the answer: out standing in his field."

Though he had only made it through eighth grade, he married a schoolteacher, Wanda Hodgkinson. They began life together without electricity in a tiny farmhouse. As a wedding present, they received indoor plumbing.

Though he lived on the outskirts of town, McClelland was quickly known throughout Burlington, volunteering to teach kids at 4-H courses and helping to start a class on shooting safety.

It was there among friends on the plains that he would start his stories. He could keep a campfire riveted with tales of nearby gunfights and yarns of the old West. As he aged, the stories became his own.

"One of the last stories he told me before he died was about a time in the fifties he went five years without a crop," John McClelland says. "They didn't have any feed, there were dust storms and a drought, and the cattle were all sold off."

"There were many a tear shed that day," Wanda says.

"He went around town and paid off all his bills and had a dollar and sixty cents left in his pocket; that's all he had to his name," John says. "He said there isn't much difference between having a dollar sixty and being dead broke, so he went to the (movie) show, he took the family to the show and spent the rest of the money.

"And when he came out of the show it was raining."

ON A SHELF AT THE Colorado State University Extension office there's a coffee cup with a hand-scrawled cattle brand, a lazy M reversed R, which around here means McClelland.

"Every once in a while he'd just stop in for coffee. He'd have a cup of coffee and put it up after he was done, and we wouldn't touch it," says Perry Brewer, an extension agent at the office. "We told him, Bob, it'll be here next time you come in."

The coffee cup will stay put.

"How do you characterize someone who's been in fifty years as a 4-H leader?" Brewer asks. "I've been around the state and I've had extension work in other states, and you don't find people like him."

So when Kit Carson County thought about refurbishing the old carousel in time for the 1976 Bicentennial, they knew where to go. In all the time McClelland lived in the area, the carousel was only run a few times a year. The animals were shoddy and the organ was busted, so the music came from old Tammy Wynette 45s on a record player.

Some folks figured they should just strip the paint off the animals and slap a few new coats on them. Others thought they should give up on the organ. Bob McClelland—along with others on the newly formed Carousel Committee—decided that if they were going to do this thing, they were going to do it right.

"When they first started, it took lots of time," Wanda McClelland says. "In the beginning I would have to drive the tractor while he was over here or out raising money."

After years of painstaking improvements by experts in the field such as Will Morton of Lakewood and Art Reblitz of Colorado Springs, the carousel was restored down to the glass eyes and horsehair. Now a national landmark, it is the oldest carousel in the nation renovated to the original paint.

Right about here, Bob McClelland would have wanted to say that there were plenty of other people along the way who made that carousel happen, and those people would want to say that it wouldn't have happened the way it did without Bob.

The McClellands eventually moved into Burlington, the last ones from the tiny nearby farming township to make the move. Bob referred to the move into the city of 3,000 as "being housebroken."

"It seemed like once we sold our cattle and our animals at the farm," Wanda says, looking at the carousel, "these became our animals to share with people."

THE GRANDKIDS ALWAYS REFERRED to the animals as "Grandpa's Carousel," but he blushed at the thought.

"He always stressed that it belonged to the people of the county," his wife says. "He would go to schools and he would say, 'It's your merry-go-round, not mine. It's yours. It belongs to all of us.'"

When thieves broke in and stole three horses and a donkey in 1981, it was Bob McClelland who persuaded the sheriff to get the FBI involved. When the theft ring was broken up, McClelland, along with a couple friends, took the senior citizens' van from nearby Flagler and personally drove to Kansas to pick the horses up, wrapping them in blankets for the way home. Then they had a parade.

Despite the security risk and concerns about damaging the precious horses, McClelland always felt that the carousel was there to be used.

"He felt really strongly about opening it all the time—anytime anyone came into town," his wife says. "(Some people) said we should have special hours when we're open. He would go and open it up every time."

His son stands near the big dog, his father's favorite animal.

"His love for this wasn't about the carousel," he says. "He loved the animals; he loved the music. But it was about the kids. The look on their faces and his face."

"You're right," Wanda says. "It was the kids."

This is about the time in the tour Bob McClelland would say the words everyone waited for:

"Let's go for a ride."

As the old organ begins its thundering, wondrous warbling, mother and son walk around the carousel, past the lion's amber eyes, past the Indian pony and the giant dog, past the fanciful horse with a fish tail. They climb into one of the intricate wooden chariots and sit next to each other.

As the animals begin to spin, they wipe their eyes and look out into the blur.

A Street Service
for a Blood Brother

Waldron Chandler Rock

THEY GATHER ON THE PAVEMENT, their grizzled faces aglow in the orange flicker of an open fire under cold stars. Rock's kind of people, in his kind of place.

"I don't normally go to memorials. I don't like 'em at all," says one of the men trying to keep warm. "But this one I got to go to, come hell or high water. Respect for Rock."

"Rock!" another man shouts, and raises his plastic cup.

For the past two decades, Waldron Rock was a fixture on the streets, parks, and foothills near Boulder. Those who didn't know him likely averted their eyes, trying not to meet his. Those who did know him say Rock's eyes kept them safe.

The people around the fire remember him as the massive Lakota Sioux Indian with the silvery black beard. They remember him as the Vietnam veteran who never talked about his service but carried his record everywhere. They remember him as a man who could fight like the end of the world and the one who would quietly give up his blanket to a stranger. They say he could have paid for his own home but slept most every night of his life outside.

"He did more for homeless people than people with homes do," says his friend Sarah Keefer.

"That's the Marine from Vietnam watching out for his buddies," says Stephen Allen.

Some of the men wear scars on their palms, the places where they cut themselves and grasped his huge hand. Tonight, his blood brothers mix with the friends who have long since left the streets but always knew where to find him.

As the memorial service continues, a man stands up and comes to the middle of the crowd.

"One word," he says, his speech slurring. "I only want to say one word."

"Ko-la," he says, once he has their attention. "In the Lakota Sioux language, that means 'friend.'"

"Ko-la. Rock."

Waldron Chandler Rock died February 11, 2001, in Longmont. He was fifty-four.

AS THE SERVICE CONTINUES, Keefer reads a eulogy filled with a history few of his friends knew — the boy before the Rock.

"Rock, a tall proud Lakota Sioux Indian, was born June 25, 1946, at Porcupine, on the Pine Ridge Reservation in South Dakota," she says. "During his younger years his family nickname was 'Scooper.' Rock played high school football. He was homecoming king his senior year in high school."

During the Vietnam War, Rock served with the Marines and would earn the Vietnam Service Medal, the Vietnam Campaign Medal, and the Republic of Vietnam Cross of Gallantry. He was shot during combat but recovered, returning home with a Purple Heart that he never showed.

After the war he eventually made it to Colorado, where he stayed the rest of his life, except for occasional road trips back home. He found his way to the streets and the bottle, and never really left either one.

According to the Boulder County Coroner's office, Rock's death was probably caused by a heart attack due to cardiovascular disease, but chronic alcoholism was listed as a contributing factor. When he died, his blood alcohol level was 0.114 percent.

"Rock was kind of a ringleader of the hardcore homeless in Boulder, these guys who've been here for twenty years or more. He was a big, tall, intimidating guy, but his heart was as big as he was tall—even bigger," says Brenda Rogers, the outreach pastor for VineLife Community Church, which organized the memorial service for Rock.

"For me personally, doing street ministry for the church, going out in the midst of the homeless into the camps, Rock was always one to support the ministry and the church, and he looked out for my safety," she says. "He defended me many times."

As Rock's friends gather around the fire, the theme of protection continues. One woman says he broke down a door one night to prevent another man from raping her. Another woman says he lent her his jacket through the winter. Using his monthly check from the U.S. Department of Veterans Affairs, he would give friends money or buy them liquor but was also known to leave sacks of groceries on the doorsteps of buddies who had since sobered up.

"One night I wound up in the ditch, passed out because I was drunk. I look up and there's this big guy grabbing me. Rock pulled me out of the ditch, picked me up, and warmed me up," says Roger Buchanan. "He gave me a blanket. I said 'Thanks' and he said, 'I been there, and it's no place for a person to be.'

"You want to write something about him? Write 'savior of the homeless,'" Buchanan says. "Write that down."

DURING HIS DECADES OF SERVICE with the Boulder Police Department, Butch Howard knew where to find Rock, and knew how to talk to him. As a Vietnam veteran and recovering alcoholic himself, Howard also knew how to listen.

"'Gentle Giant' comes to mind. He respected authority. We treated him with respect and he treated us with respect. To be honest with you, I liked the guy," Howard says.

"He had two strikes against him, maybe three. Alcoholism, being a Native American, and a Vietnam vet," he says. "Vietnam didn't make him an alcoholic; it probably just guaranteed it would happen."

Though he was diagnosed with post-traumatic stress disorder, Rock never kept up with the treatment that may have helped him. He spent many nights in the Alcohol Recovery Center; a few years ago he was convicted of felony menacing and spent time in prison.

"I think the guy got screwed by himself," Howard says. "He would get drunk and stupid. ... But by what was going on in his mind, he was just bluffing. He did a lot of time in jail that he really didn't deserve."

Howard has attended countless memorial services for the guys he used to see on the street. He goes to the services for their memory and his own.

"To be honest, I'm very selfish. When it happens, it just kind of reinforces my own lifestyle. It keeps me sober," he says. "Because there but for the grace of God go I."

AS THE MEMORIAL SERVICE ENDS, Alex McCannon borrows a guitar from one of the church singers and begins the song "St. James Infirmary," a song about a man in a bar mourning the death of his loved one and reflecting on his own mortality.

"I thought it was an appropriate song," says McCannon, who has seen his own share of buddies die on the streets. Rock called McCannon "Music Man" in Lakota.

"I play it for all my dead friends," he says after a while, then picks up the guitar and repeats the last lyric:

> I want six gamblers to be my pallbearers
> six chorus girls to sing me a song
> and put a jazz band on my hearse wagon
> just to raise some hell as we roll along.

As they gather closer to the fire to keep warm, some of the men continue to share the Lakota words they learned from Rock. Others repeat Bible verses and poems. Some go off into the bushes for the jug.

"He's in a better place now," says one of the men.

"Of course he's in a better place," says another.

"He's up there with all our friends," the man says.

"Rock's up there with all our dead brothers."

Appreciating Values
in Aspen

Warren Conner

THE HOUSE STANDS IN QUIET DEFIANCE, at the center of a stereotype.

A miner's lamp hangs from the front porch, near a brass plate etched with the same name that's hung there since they started delivering the mail here. The name was here when the house was used as a miner's cottage; the family name was here even before then. The home's fraying white wood is covered in places with painted tin, patched like an old pair of jeans.

Less than a block away, on Aspen's pedestrian mall, doors beckon to Christian Dior and Gucci and The Gap, where a spandex-clad woman walks inside leading a giant poodle wearing a faux-leopard skin collar. Across the street from the little white house, there's an upscale restaurant; on another side are a bank and condominiums. SUVs whiz past the old carport that barely protects a rusty orange 1972 VW Beetle.

When Warren Conner was born, the whole block was made up of the little homes now officially described as "representative of a typical Aspen Victorian miner's cottage." These days, the little white home is one of the last ones standing—a gingerbread house long since gone stale.

"He lived the first three years of his life around the corner," says Claude Conner, as he stands in front of his brother Warren's small house. "He lived the last seventy-seven right here."

In a town where everybody's business can mean big business, Warren Conner knew everybody's business and filed it away. After more than fifty years in public service, after living nearly every hour of his life on the same square block, he knew all about appreciating values.

"Right here, right in Aspen, right on this corner. That's where he was happiest. He had many opportunities to sell it and go into a condominium," his brother says. "He always said 'No, I want to stay right here in this little house.'"

Warren Conner died April 15, 2001, in Aspen. He was eighty.

THEY USED TO SAY THAT ASPEN was a ghost town after the silver bust in the late 1800s. Margaret Conner always had something to say about that.

"If it was a ghost town," Warren's mother once told a reporter, "I was one of the ghosts."

Warren's grandparents—the Conners and Harringtons—emigrated from Ireland in the mid-1800s. After mining for decades, his grandfather served as the undersheriff of Aspen, beginning more than a century of public service tied to the family.

Warren was born in 1920, in a home near the county courthouse. Three years later, the family moved around the corner to the house where Warren would spend the rest of his life.

The house at 534 Hopkins was moved from its original spot near Aspen Mountain in 1908 and placed downtown near other similar cottages. These days, some people look down their noses at the dilapidated buildings they call "miner's shacks." The people who call them that never lived in one.

Warren spent much of his childhood playing in the places he would later work. He often visited his grandfather at the courthouse, where the Conner kids would play cops and robbers using the real jail. He also helped out at the neighboring Armory building, where he shoveled coal into the furnace alongside his father (the building now holds city offices).

Warren graduated from Aspen High in 1938 and enlisted in the Navy, but the military rejected him because of a heart problem. That weak heart kept Warren Conner from strenuous activity his whole life, but it didn't faze his work ethic. Conner soon took a job at the courthouse where he already knew every hallway blindfolded. In 1947 he was named deputy county treasurer, and in 1949 he became deputy county assessor. He walked one block to work at the courthouse each day until his retirement in 1991 and continued to stop by even after that.

"He was very good with detail. He knew every piece of property in the county," says Claude Conner, who remembers many trips with Warren into the mountains, where his brother could recite property histories from when they were mining claims up to modern sites for million-dollar homes for movie stars.

From the condos sprouting across from his porch and the escalating figures in his tax assessment books, Conner watched

Aspen transform. Though he didn't complain about the growth, he did regret seeing so many old-timers move away and wondered why the new residents kept missing the slow gear.

"As far as Aspen today, one of my heartfelt wishes would be for people who live and work here to be able to afford to live here and not go banging down the highway to go home," he told the *Aspen Times* in 1997. "Another wish would be for people to slow down for others in the crosswalks. People are always in such a hurry nowadays."

In Conner Memorial Park near the old white house, a towering spruce tree shades the picnic benches. Warren Conner planted that tree some sixty years ago, after finding the sapling up near Conundrum Creek. He spent plenty of time hiking the trails and creeks for the rest of his life, bird watching with friends, or angling in places where the fish seemed to know he was coming and didn't seem to mind.

In his spare time, Conner would often head up to the old mining claims, collecting the rocks he eventually parlayed into a collection that spanned the history of the area and its mines. The rocks were displayed for years in a local museum. Now they hide in boxes in Warren Conner's garage.

"He went out to the museum one day and they had his rock collection pushed out of the spot where it used to be and put back into a back room," Claude Conner says. "Warren said 'Why is this?' And they told him mining's not important to the town anymore; it's all skiing. So he got his rock collection out of there.

"That's too bad, but that's what happens," Claude says. "Sometimes people just don't know."

The Conner family eventually bought two houses next to the old white one; the patch where they used to garden is now Conner Memorial Park. The homes have since been declared historic landmarks.

Warren Conner never married. He lived with his parents in the white house, caring for them until his father died eighteen years ago and his mother died in September of 2000. Soon afterwards, Warren's health began to fail.

As long as he was physically able, Conner attended daily Mass at St. Mary's Catholic Church. The house where he was born stood across from the church's front door; the house he lived in the last seventy-seven years looked at the church's back door. When new priests would come to head the church, they would often get the key from Conner.

Six priests oversaw Conner's funeral service, some from St. Benedict's Monastery in Snowmass, where Conner had helped the monks acquire their property. He was buried in Red Butte cemetery— a place where he sometimes walked among the headstones, reciting the histories of the names on the rocks and conjuring images of the places they lived.

As Conner's funeral service ended—just as friends and family finished the last hymn—a siren rang through the town and into the cemetery, as it does every day at noon.

"Someone said, 'How traditional. Right at the end of the service, the siren went off,'" Claude Conner says.

"They used to blow the siren for the miners at the end of each shift. They blew the siren when the shift was over."

Mr. and Mrs. Marshal

Jimmy and Vera Griffith

IN FRONT OF THE GRIFFITH HOME on Griffith Street at the edge of Nederland, residents pick through the remains of the Griffiths' lives: boxes of rocks, dusty car headlights, rusty battery chargers, and piles of yellowing yardsticks. Old televisions sit near silent transistor radios and rotary dial telephones.

The Griffiths aren't around for the yard sale. Vera Griffith died just over a week ago, and then Jimmy Griffith said he couldn't live without her.

"I didn't want to do this," says Betty Kornegay, who organized the sale. "But there's so much stuff. I didn't know what else to do."

Kornegay is Vera Griffith's daughter. She and her husband arrived after her mother was taken to Boulder Community Hospital on June 27, 1998. Griffith, eighty-four, died that day, with the family at her side.

"We took care of everything with Mother, and we were set to go back to Nevada on Thursday," Kornegay says.

"Then Jimmy went and did that thing."

Kornegay takes a long drag on a cigarette and again surveys the yard. Nearby, chunks of toilet plumbing sit near coffee cans full of nails and a Christmas wreath, still encrusted with lights.

"All these treasures," she says.

VERA WAS BORN IN LONGMONT but moved to Nederland in 1959 after she met Jimmy, who was town marshal. Most everyone in town soon recognized Vera's face from her waitress jobs at several local bars and restaurants. Though the couple never officially married, they had the kind of fun of which legends are made. Unfortunately, friends say with a wink, most of those legends don't belong in the newspaper.

Sometimes, Jimmy and Vera would sit on the porch of the old drugstore and people would call them "Matt and Kitty," after the two main characters in the TV western "Gunsmoke." Some folks even called Vera "Mrs. Marshal," thanks to a feistiness that far outmatched that of her husband.

When Jimmy wasn't working, they were together. Even when he was working, they were together. After he quit the marshal job, he headed up maintenance at the Alexander Dawson school in Lafayette, then served as foreman for the Boulder County Road District.

In the mid-1990s, the Griffiths presided as grand marshals of the annual Nederland Old-Timers Parade, riding proudly down Main Street in a Model T Ford. At this year's annual Fourth of July picnic, two horses clopped down the street riderless, in the Griffiths' memory.

As friends pick through the things in the Griffiths' front yard, many say they were saddened by what Jimmy did but they weren't necessarily shocked. Jimmy always said he didn't know what he would do if Vera went first.

One woman at the yard sale says she had a dream in which Vera's in heaven.

"Vera looks over and says, 'Jimmy, you're here too?' "

JIMMY GRIFFITH WAS BORN in the house his father built, along the road that would later become Griffith Street. Back then, Jimmy's father was the town marshal, trying to keep the peace among the miners. A few decades later, Jimmy would wear the marshal's star, trying to keep the peace among Nederland's newest residents.

Like almost every man in Nederland at the time, Griffith started out working in the mines. When he was named the town's sole law-enforcement officer, he rarely wore a uniform, since he also served as street commissioner, water superintendent, and cemetery caretaker.

During the infamous "hippie invasion" of Nederland in the late 1960s, Griffith tried a more diplomatic approach than the heavy-handed tactics favored by many in town.

"Some members of the town council wanted me to do something about the kids—run 'em out of town or beat 'em up or something. I just never felt like doing anything like that," he said in a newspaper interview.

Even during those turbulent times, says longtime resident Brownlee Guyer, Marshal Griffith kept his cool.

"He was a quiet sort of a fella, but he was good at his work," Guyer says. "We get some guys that get star-itis, the ones that like to show their authority, and he wasn't like that.

"He was one of those little-but-mighty guys. He was a swell fella."

On the day Jimmy died, Guyer was headed up to Griffith Street to check on his good friend.

When Guyer saw the police cars, he figured he was ten minutes too late.

WHEN JIMMY'S FATHER BUILT the house where Jimmy was born, it was surrounded by hills frequented only by miners.

These days, the Griffith house is flanked by the town school bus barn and a mobile home park. The home is still heated by wood- and coal-burning stoves. Only recently did Jimmy turn the pantry closet into a working bathroom.

As Nederland moved slowly forward, Jimmy and Vera kept their feet—and their hearts—in the past. In his closet, Jimmy kept his old Navy uniform. He kept all his police records and old newspapers dating back to 1930. He even saved old paycheck stubs from his father. In the yard sits a box of decades-old padlocks—most of them missing the key.

Betty Kornegay says she tried to convince her mother and Jimmy to move out of the Griffith Street home to live in California. Jimmy would have none of it. He was too worried about what might happen to the house and all their things.

As the couple's friends from their own generation died, Jimmy worried that they would be the last of the old-timers left. Even so, they chose to stay in the only town the couple ever knew.

As some of the yard-sale customers gaze in amazement at the collection, longtime Boulder resident Ollie Shepherd surveys the Griffiths' yard.

"That's what comes from living in one place all your life," he says.

VERA GRIFFITH'S ARTIFICIAL HIP was supposed to last ten years, but it wound up lasting nineteen. When it cracked, her health went downhill quickly. At eighty-four years old, the pain was too much. Kornegay remembers leaving the hospital after her mother's death. "Afterwards, we sat outside the hospital, and I said I needed a cigarette. Jimmy hadn't smoked for years, but he said, 'Could I have one?'"

On the drive back up Boulder Canyon, Jimmy remained calm. He said he wanted to have Vera's body cremated so that when he died he could have his ashes mixed with hers.

Four days later, he wrote a note to his stepdaughter and her husband.

Dear Benny and Betty, thank you for everything. I'm sorry to do this to you, but I just can't live without Vera.

Jimmy Griffith then walked around the corner of the house where he was born and shot himself in the head. He was seventy-six.

As she takes another drag off her cigarette, Kornegay surveys the dwindling possessions in the yard and points to a field above the little house on Griffith Street.

"After (Vera) died, Jimmy took me up there and showed me a nice little meadow. He said that in the springtime it bloomed with beautiful columbines. So that's where we put the ashes," she says.

"He said that's where they wanted to be. So that's where they are."

The Cowboy on the Roof

William Lyman Davies

INSIDE THE DINER WHERE EVERYTHING REFLECTS, Brent Davies gazes into the copper mirror.

"You can't find these anywhere anymore," he says to the image of himself. "I think they make you look better."

That's Brent's last name on the thirty-six-foot tall sign outside the restaurant—as in "Davies' Chuck Wagon Diner." Near the name beckons the seventeen-foot cowboy, an enormous homage to the past, wearing a neon apron and a two-foot smile.

"I gotta tell you that sign was my dad's idea," Davies says. "He knew he had to keep the western motif; he had to have that cowboy up there."

It was also his dad's idea to put the life-size fiberglass horse on top of the stainless steel diner, old West above the new. Actually, just about everything about this place was William Lyman Davies' idea, and most of them are just like that mirror. Most of them, you can't find anywhere anymore.

"Everyone thought he was crazy when he put that horse on the roof," Brent Davies says. "But that was my dad."

Since the day he set up the gleaming restaurant in the sparsely populated area on West Colfax Avenue—more than a decade before the area around it would be called Lakewood—Davies knew what he wanted. He had planned it most of his life.

The diner's newest owner, Dwayne Clark, plops himself down in a booth across from Brent Davies, and the two share stories in a place built for them. By now, the word has gotten around to most of the regulars. William Lyman Davies died March 27, 2000. He was eighty-three.

"There are still a lot of people who remember him. A lot of the old timers come in to talk about the old times," Clark says. "They talk about the changes, too. A lot of changes in Lakewood."

As he looks around inside the diner, Clark says he'll never forget the lessons he learned from the man who put the horse on the roof.

"My dad knew your dad for years," he says to Brent Davies. "The main thing I learned from his father was the personal touch. You have to be out here. That's what his father was known for. If a baby was crying, he'd pick the baby up and walk around the restaurant with it so the parents could eat. You don't see that much anymore."

A while back, the city tried to get Clark to lower the sign and get rid of the horse. The city lost. Since then, Clark says he's tried to keep everything the way Davies designed it, the way people remember it. As much as you can these days.

Inside the diner where everything reflects, the two men look into the copper mirror.

"These mirrors do make you look better," Clark says. "They make you look younger."

WILLIAM LYMAN DAVIES HAD THE DREAM long before he first came to Colorado. When he finally settled in the Rockies, the dream had a recipe.

Davies was raised on a ranch in Utah, and as a teenager he worked his way up to manager of the local Walgreens restaurant— back when they used to have restaurants in drugstores. During the next twenty years he was manager of all the company's restaurants in the country, and by then the dream had a thick foundation—a place all his own.

"He traveled all across the country and began to collect a list of favorite dishes from each restaurant," Brent Davies says. "We still have that book of recipes. I don't know what we'll do with it; each recipe is for 100 to 200 people."

In his two decades with Walgreens, Davies and his wife Helen moved from his home state of Utah to Idaho, Colorado, Kentucky, Ohio, and Illinois. In 1957, he took every penny he had saved and threw it into an empty lot at 9495 W. Colfax Avenue. At the time, Colfax was the only way to get from Denver to Golden. Inside that patch of grass, Davies saw shimmering steel and a giant cowboy.

Davies had his eye on a prefabricated restaurant from the aptly named Mountain View Diners in New Jersey. To transport the building by railroad to Denver and open it would cost nearly $200,000. In the 1950s, it was everything Davies had, and more.

"I remember sitting in the bank with him," Brent Davies says. "I was just a little kid but I remember the banker telling my dad he was crazy for trying to open a restaurant that far out of town, that he'd never make it."

Today the diner still seats fifty-seven. The menu was, as Lyman Davies had dreamed, a collection of his favorites—from the malted waffles he loved from back east to the fried chicken he once tasted at a little place in Kentucky.

"I remember standing back there with Colonel Sanders, learning how to fry chicken—he was a character, the beard and everything," Brent Davies says. "I think we were the first to sell his chicken outside of Kentucky."

Just as he had Colonel Harland Sanders personally instruct the family on his original recipe, Davies always wanted the best. When he learned that the only way to buy the special malt for his favorite waffles was by the truckload, he bought a truckload, and then got to selling it.

"He worked 6 a.m. to 3 p.m., and then usually me or my brother would come in to do the evening shift," Brent says. "I can remember him working twenty-four to thirty hours at a time when we first opened."

As the diner remained open twenty-four hours a day, the family members took shifts, spending much of their time together at their shiny home away from home.

"When a customer came in (a second time), the waitress had to remember their name," Brent Davies remembers. "It was required. (William Davies) dwelled on that, the personal aspect. That epitomized my dad, because he was quite a personable character. He was also a jokester. When you came in a third time, you were likely to get a rubber egg on your plate."

A BLOCK AWAY FROM THE STAINLESS STEEL stands one of the only places nearby that was here before Davies' diner. Inside is another man with his name on the sign outside.

H.W. "Scat" Scatterday, proprietor of Scatterday's Lumber, has had his share of meals at the diner in the past forty years.

"As you can tell," he says, smiling and patting his belly.

The diner is one of the reasons Scatterday became a city councilman.

"They started coming down on us and they made us change our sign. Then they started coming down hard on the cowboy, and I said, 'OK, that's enough.' We've got to have some history to count on," Scatterday says. "The feeling is, 'If it's more than ten years old, tear it down.' These are the same people who go over to Europe to look at all the old buildings."

Davies and Scatterday sit in Scatterday's office and talk about their fathers, the old times, and new.

"When the diner opened the only thing that was between here and Golden was Horton's gas station," Davies says. "I think it would be about where the Burger King is today."

"Nope," Scatterday says. "I think it's over there where Circuit City is."

ON THE DINER'S PATIO, a woman dressed in shorts and a fanny pack holds a camera to her face, framing her husband and child.

"Do you have the horse in the picture?" the man asks.

In 1970, the Davies family closed the diner for the first time to attend the funeral of William Davies' father. Before leaving, they had to hire a locksmith—the first time they needed locks on the doors.

In the late 1970s, William Davies' health began to deteriorate after more than two decades behind the counter, so he sold the diner. He continued to raise horses and ride them with the Jefferson County Sheriff's Posse, and was still known to pop inside the diner to say hello. In the 1980s, a stroke ended those days.

"If you wanted to hit him where it hurts, that's what it was," Brent Davies says. "It took away his speech. With all that locked up inside, all the people he wanted to talk to ... it hurt."

At a table in the shadow of the cowboy sign, eighty-eight-year-old Julio Zamagni says the legacy of the man remains.

"He was a cook, but he was more of a PR person—very affable, very outgoing," Zamagni says, as he chomps down a burger. "He was a horseman, and anyone who loves horses loves people."

Over the past few decades, the diner has been featured in a couple of movies, a Colorado Lottery commercial, and a Lucky Strikes cigarette commercial. In 1997, after lobbying by the Lakewood Historical Society, the diner was entered into the National Register of Historic Places by the U.S. Department of the Interior—only the ninth such restaurant in the country to receive the honor. By then, the diner's first owner had moved back to Utah, where he lived his last years on a ranch of his own. Before he died, William Davies knew the cowboy was safe.

Inside the diner, Brent Davies and Dwayne Clark walk through the kitchen and past a grill packed with sizzling bacon, steak, and artfully splattered French toast. Together, they walk into the basement and look up at the seams where the diner was joined together forty-three years ago.

"You have some new retro-diners coming in, but they're not like this," Clark says. "They're not original."

The two men stand there, looking up toward the diner overhead. The lunch rush is just about to begin.

"Well, Dwayne," Davies says, "some things don't change."

"Nope," Clark says. "Some don't."

Another Terrible Year for the Soil

Gregory D. Harris

BARBARA HARRIS STANDS NEAR ten acres of fallow winter wheat, trying to see the dry, brown landscape through her husband's clear blue eyes.

"You can see how dry it is," she says. "You know that it's the worst year here. Some say it's the worst in a hundred years," she says. "Terrible, terrible year."

If her husband were here right now, he would be looking up in the sky, at the clouds gathering over Sleeping Ute Mountain, confident that they carried rain. He would be out there, alone, in the fields where he spent his entire life, talking to the sky.

"If he saw clouds he absolutely expected rain. And the same with snow in the wintertime," she says. "He'd come in and I'd say, 'Well, did you give your orders to mother nature?' And he would smile."

When the couple built their home here in Marvel in 1985, people told them it would be tough to make it as farmers out on the dry land southwest of Durango. He knew those people were right, and he didn't care.

"He would stand here on the deck, just surveying his kingdom, looking out," she says. "And he loved it. Just loved it."

In a few weeks, Harris and her children will walk out to that fallow wheat field and open a metal box containing her husband's ashes.

"Each field has a name, usually named after the owner or the past owner, and even if there are two or three generations afterwards they keep the name," she says, looking out at the area where she plans to scatter the ashes.

"This field is called 'The Homeplace.'"

Gregory D. Harris died on his farm on April 24, 2002, of malignant melanoma. He was forty-nine.

THERE ARE PLENTY OF DATES in Greg Harris' life that most people would call significant—his birthday, the year he graduated from college, the date he was married. For the shy, burly, fair-skinned man who grew up with his hands in the soil, the best year of his life was, without a doubt, 1976.

"He hit a lick. It was his first year farming all by himself, and he hit a huge lick," Barbara Harris says. "Everything went right. He had the fall moisture to get the crop up. He had a winter snow, spring rain, and doggonit he had a wonderful yield. And he thought every year after would be a similar situation."

She walks up to the red and white Case Agri-King tractor he bought that year and treated like his child for the next twenty-five.

"He kind of got stuck in time. People go back to the years that they were the most comfortable and had the best time, and Greg never gave up raising another good crop," his wife says. "And when you look at his wheat rotation this year that is supposed to be cut in July, you'll see that there's nothing there."

For Harris, the drought was just another challenge—one he swore he could overcome, no matter what anyone else told him. And he would do it his way.

"He did not dress like a farmer. He dressed in bright orange Converse high-top tennis shoes, shorts, and T-shirts," Barbara Harris says. "He didn't wear overalls or cowboy shirts; he rarely wore cowboy boots."

It was a self-awareness that started early. As a boy, he charmed the family with his dry, shy sense of humor, then went on to graduate with honors and a degree in political science from Fort Lewis College—all the while living and working on the family farm.

Though as a young man he partied hard—often too hard—as he grew older he channeled his energy into the land, and for the second half of his life he rarely drank anything stronger than coffee. On the rare vacation, he loved going to museums around the Four Corners area, where he would often spend hours learning about other people's pasts, while trying to keep his own from vanishing.

"There used to be businesses here in Marvel. He went to school here. They even had a bank," Harris says of the tiny town her husband watched fade. "When he was in college he did a paper on the people of old Marvel. He interviewed all the old-timers. And it was very important to him, that he was preserving some of that history before it disappeared."

As more and more farmers gave up, he refused. In the winters he worked construction for a while, then worked for the city of

Durango—all to help subsidize his passion for the farm. He tried livestock, even raising trout for a while, but always returned to the crops.

"Agriculture is not easy at all, and out here it's even more difficult. But Greg was so dedicated to agriculture," Harris says. "He was just tireless."

She stops in the field and pauses for a minute, working things out in her head. "He was such a realist most of his life. He wouldn't even go to see a science fiction movie because it wasn't about real life.

"It's kind of sad, but as realistic as Greg was, this (kind of farming) wasn't always realistic. It's a dichotomy. A dichotomy," she says. "He kept thinking he'd hit that lick again one of these years.

"He never gave up."

BEHIND THE BAR L-H CATTLE BRAND on a sign a few miles from Greg Harris' home, his parents remember a boy who serenaded the seedlings.

"When the crops came in he was so happy, he had a little song he would sing, and a little dance," says his mother, Angie Harris, as she starts to sing: "Look at these beans, Pa look at that corn. Look at these beans, Pa, look at that corn.' And he'd dance around his little jig."

"You know, I learned determination from him," says his father, Donald Harris, who left the farm to work in the oil fields for a while, but like his son never fully gave it up. "I learned that if you're determined you can do OK."

On a hillside near another of Greg Harris' favorite fields, his father is hard at work building a memorial to his son. Nearby, several dozen acres of hay continue to struggle. It was the last field that Greg fertilized before the skin cancer took hold; he died about two months after the diagnosis.

"This is the worst year I can remember. A full-fledged drought," his father says. "Everything's going downhill now. It's in the doldrums.

"But you know, Greg wouldn't a paid any attention to it," he says. "He woulda just been out there, getting his land ready.

"Ready for another crop."

Living With the Risk

Tom Dunwiddie and Monika Eldridge

WHEN RANGERS FROM YOSEMITE National Park found the rolls of film in the car, they hoped to learn something about the bodies at the bottom of Middle Cathedral Rock. When the film was developed, the snapshots dripped with adrenaline.

In the pictures, the two climbers hug walls of granite throughout the park, alternatively serious and smiling, hundreds of feet above the ground. Many climbers would take weeks to climb all the places in those photos, yet the film from the car spanned only five days.

It wasn't that Tom Dunwiddie and Monika Eldridge were in a hurry, they told their friends. This was just their natural pace.

When he pressed his cheek to the warm face of a rock, Dunwiddie felt it down to his nerves. A world-renowned neuroscientist, he found relaxation while dangling from cliffs, his synapses firing in complete concentration.

In a different way, Eldridge also found knowledge in the alternating stress and peace of the sheer rock faces. A nuclear and solar engineer, she spent the last part of her life searching for renewable power, hoping to protect the places she loved.

Away from the climbs, Dunwiddie, 49, and Eldridge, 40, led separate lives. Their friendship was linked by their knowledge of the ropes and anchors, by the understanding of each other's strengths and the desire to make another ascent.

About a year before their trip to Yosemite, Dunwiddie had thought about giving up climbing after a friend's close call in Utah. He should have known he would return to the rocks. Inside his lab at the University of Colorado, his specialty was addiction.

At about 1 p.m. on July 12, 2001, a fisherman on Yosemite's Merced Lake heard the sound of rocks breaking loose and looked up to see the two climbers falling, still tied together. Their bodies collided with rocks as they fell more than 800 feet, and they died as the air rushed past.

ON TOM DUNWIDDIE'S KINDERGARTEN report card, he received one poor mark:

"Doesn't nap well," the teacher wrote.

The family took outdoor trips in their native Wisconsin from the time Tom was a baby. When he was only twenty months old, the family took a canoe trip together, and by the time Tom was walking, he was hiking. When they weren't outside, he and his siblings played chamber music as a quartet, with Tom on violin. The music took a backseat when he left for college, however—the orchestra group met on the same evening as the climbing club.

Though he attended college at the University of Wisconsin and University of California, he spent much of his spare time in the mountains of Colorado. At school he concentrated on research involving how nerves send information to the brain. He put the theories into practice while backcountry skiing, mountain biking, and climbing. When a chance arrived in 1978 to take a postdoctoral position at the University of Colorado Health Sciences Center, there was never any question.

It wasn't long before he made an impression on the professors—and not only with his depth of intelligence and research. Instead of spending every waking moment in the lab, he taught the scientists to telemark ski and took them to mountains they had previously only seen through windows. During a brain research conference in Keystone, he passed up the condo where his colleagues stayed, choosing instead to camp in his own snow cave.

Dunwiddie's postdoctoral mentor Barry Hoffer remembers a time when the two went to the Boulder campus to use some equipment in the engineering building. Hoffer soon saw a security guard running to the side of the building, trying to catch the young scientist.

"Tom climbed the CU engineering building on the *outside*," Hoffer said. "Twenty feet above the floor he taps on the glass and comes in through 'the easy way.'"

In 1981, Dunwiddie was given his own lab at the Health Sciences Center, where his name would find its way onto hundreds of research papers—many of them concerning the brain's reaction to drugs and reasons for drug abuse. (Dunwiddie's only stimulant—excluding the outdoors—came from a collection of imported black teas.)

After the announcement of his death, e-mail condolences poured in from around the world. At his funeral service in Denver's City Park on July 27, colleagues who had flown in from as far as Sweden remembered his legacy to the field—and to the mountains.

"I respect his science," Hoffer said. "But more importantly, I respect his approach to science."

WHEN MONIKA ELDRIDGE WAS THREE years old, her parents put up a chain link fence around their new home in Tennessee. The day the fence was completed, Monika climbed over it.

"I could not build a treehouse that was safe from her," said her older brother, Owen. "Whether it was one in the yard or one hidden in the woods, she would find it and climb it."

She had always dreamed of becoming an astronaut but was told she was too short (just over five feet tall) and had less-than-perfect vision. That didn't stop her from graduating from the University of Delaware in 1982 with a degree in mechanical and aerospace engineering. Soon after graduation she found a job with Consumers Power Company (now Consumers Energy Company) in Michigan and was the first woman in the state certified to run a nuclear power plant.

Despite her success, she told friends she was bored staring at control panels all day, that she found the real challenges outdoors. In 1990, she left the literal seat of power and headed for Boulder, where she bought a house in the shadow of the mountains.

For Eldridge, the Flatirons were dull pink magnets, drawing her to their base for sunrise runs every day. After a few hours at work with an energy consulting firm, she would take off on her mountain bike and ride up Flagstaff Mountain during her lunch break.

In 1999, she formed her own consulting firm, Competitive Utility Strategies, looking for better ways to use energy and concentrating on renewable energy sources such as wind and solar power. She worked from home, where she built a climbing wall in the basement.

THE GRANITE OF MIDDLE CATHEDRAL ROCK stretches more than 1,000 feet from the bottom of the Yosemite Valley. The climb up the Direct North Buttress is considered an advanced intermediate climb—not an extremely difficult one but long and involved. By all accounts, Middle Cathedral Rock was well within the range of the pair's climbing expertise.

According to a report on the accident by park investigators, "It appears that the man was leading the climb and the female was belaying at the time" of the fall. "He took a leader fall and the force of arresting the fall pulled the belay anchors from their attachment point."

"The one thing that everyone agrees on is that more than one thing went wrong," said Dunwiddie's wife, Nancy, who also works as a researcher and professor at the Health Sciences Center.

After police told her the news, she thought about going to Yosemite to see the rock but then decided against it. She may go one day, she says, but not yet. Though she spent most of the past twenty years near Tom, she didn't share her husband's passion for technical climbing. She hiked with him, she skied with him, and worked near him, but rarely strapped on the gear.

"I don't have to be challenged the way he did," she said. "To relax, Tom had to have all his faculties engaged in that sport."

In their house, Dunwiddie built a climbing wall stretching from the basement to the attic. Another climbing wall in the garage occasionally snagged the car's right-hand mirror. At the couple's cabin in the mountains, he would practice climbing on the beams that supported the house and train on the branches of elm trees. In winter he would stand outside on the porch railing and do backflips into the snow.

"Someone asked me once if I'd ever tried to get Tom to stop climbing," Nancy said. "I said I don't think he would have been the same person. He was like a moth to a candle."

DURING HER LIFE, ELDRIDGE occasionally scribbled down her thoughts, along with life lessons. On one page that her family found, she had written "My Philosophy," then attempted to figure out what it was.

Why am I here on earth? I don't know but I can make the most of it, she wrote. *I feel as if there is a special reason for me being here but I can't seem to figure out what it is. I feel as if I am supposed to do something great and noble. I just don't know what that is.*

As he walked in her backyard, her friend Leland Keller said he has an idea of the answer.

"Her philosophy was largely based on balance, acceptance, and doing what you can do for others," Keller said. "She lived it. She didn't fake it. High integrity. Very authentic. Genuine, loving person."

In the past year, she had signed on to work with the Hopi Indian Nation to expand solar power on the Arizona reservation through a company (majority owned by the Hopis) called Native Sun. The day she left for Yosemite, she called her partner, finalizing the plans for the company and its investors.

"We're going to move forward with the project, but I figure I'm going to have to bring in at least two and possibly as many as four people to replace the expertise she had," said Rick Gilliam, her partner in the project. "She was certainly talented. But the energy and enthusiasm she had was infectious."

As it turned out, her family says, she never needed to question her place in the world. Among her things, they found another handwritten guide to life:

Live each day to the fullest
Get the most from each hour, each day
And each age of your life.

Be yourself, but be your best self
Dare to be different
And follow your own star.

Don't be afraid to be happy
Enjoy what is beautiful
Love with all your heart and soul
Believe that those you love
Love you.

When you are faced with decision
Make that decision as wisely as possible then forget it.
The moment of absolute certainty never arrives.

And above all, remember that
God helps those who help themselves
Act as if everything depended upon it
And pray as if everything depended upon God.

IN LATE 1999, NANCY DUNWIDDIE started saving her husband's answering machine messages. He had called after a friend was injured by a falling rock in Utah and had to be rescued by helicopter. It was the first time in two decades that Tom called to report an accident. Although he said he would stop climbing, he was back on the rocks within months.

His last message from Yosemite was typically upbeat.

"At the end (of the message) he said, 'Have fun with all your buddies,'" she said. "He wasn't one to say 'I love you' or 'I'm missing you' on the phone. You could read between the lines. It was just the fact that he called."

In the scientific community, they were known as a model couple, two people who could work so close and so hard, yet could leave it at the lab, escaping together on the slopes and trails.

Sometimes he would joke about the pictures she took. While his were often extreme shots of skiers or climbers, or long views of mountain ranges, she would often take multiple close-up photos of wildflowers.

"More of Nancy's flower pictures," he would say with a smile when showing off the slides.

In those last photos her husband ever took, Nancy saw something the rangers couldn't have understood.

"In that last roll, he had taken about a dozen pictures of flowers," she remembered. "I was looking at the pictures with his sister and she pointed to the flowers.

"She said, 'See. He was thinking of you.'"

The Man Who Spoke Horse

Keith Hagler

"HUP!"

In one syllable he said everything that needed to be said, and those he cared about took notice. Their ears pricked, their big eyes locked, and they found the deep-voiced man who could read every twitch.

"He was a man beyond belief when it came to knowing how to interact with a horse," says Rex Walker of Sombrero Ranches, based in Boulder. "I think they communicated with each other. Somehow he knew what they were going to do."

During his life, Keith Hagler met a lot of people and traded thousands of horses. Sometimes he remembered a person's face. He never forgot a horse.

"Keith wasn't a horse whisperer as they are known today, but you could see the connection between him and any horse the first time they met. They both knew," wrote his friend, Lonnie Mantle. "Keith spoke horse and the language of the West."

As she sits in their home south of Longmont, his wife looks over Mantle's condolence letter. Outside, her husband's best friends graze in the sunset.

"I think I'm going to put that on his gravestone," Karen Hagler says.

"He spoke horse."

Keith Hagler died in Longmont on October 11, 2001, after a massive stroke. He was sixty-three.

HE LEARNED TO WALK around horses; they taught him how to grow up. He was born in Fort Collins, but his family soon moved to Nebraska, where he was the short, new kid, the only one who still rode his horse to school. Even as he grew taller than six feet and bulked up from the work, he still preferred a horse's company to almost any human.

As a teenager he spent his summers with his brother on a ranch near Walden and knew he belonged in those pastures. The day he graduated from high school, he got on a bus and came to Colorado. After training horses and trading them throughout the West, he met a guy named Rex Walker at a horse sale in Denver, and the two struck up a friendship.

"He had a talent with horses beyond anyone I've ever known in my whole life," says Walker, who, in 1959 started Sombrero Ranches, an operation that began with a few head of horses and later expanded to thousands.

As a partner in the ranch, Hagler traveled from Canada to Mexico, finding horses the company would train and rent to scouting organizations, riding stables, television commercials, and movie productions. He also picked and managed the horses for the massive Tucson, Arizona, rodeo parade; often he was the one driving a team down the main street. When he ran into a horse years after he sold it, they always seemed to recognize each other.

"He knew every horse," Walker says. "He knew how old it was, he knew its disposition, he knew its good and bad points."

When the men got together, there was only one topic of conversation.

"Our whole life is centered around our horses. We didn't talk about anything but horses," Walker says. "That's what we liked. And he was worse about it than I am."

Hagler was never very verbal—few people ever got much more than "yep" or "nope" out of him—but he had to deal with a lot of people during the job. He once said that when he got frustrated with clueless tourists or movie people, he would just look in their eyes and see the dollar signs. When he looked in the big, dark eyes of a horse, he saw his reflection.

"The only time he was happy was when he was with the horses. He took better care of the horses than himself," Walker says. "That's probably one reason he's dead."

By the end, he limped along on a leg that never really healed right after a horse kick shattered it. He lived with cracked ribs, various broken bones, and two torn rotator cuffs that he endured for a year before finally going to the doctor. Still, his muscles remained tough as a fencepost. When friends from the stable tried to throw him into the horse trough for his birthday, he fought off every one.

Along with the horses, he helped train hundreds of boys who came to the ranch—many of them who had gotten crossways with their families and needed straightening out. Hagler worked them hard but gave them the same respect he afforded the horses.

When pressed to find a fault with his partner, Walker has to think a minute.

"He was hard on a truck," he says finally. "He always had a dent in his truck or had his shirt tore. Other than that he got along pretty good."

AT THE BAR OPEN BOX K RANCH south of Longmont, Karen Hagler wanders among the paint horses the whole family helped raise.

"They probably don't know he's gone," she says. "This is the time of year he would be gone anyway, working over on the Western Slope."

Karen met Keith in Arizona in 1974 while he managed a stable there. At the time, she taught riding lessons. They married thirty days after their first date; they had the most important thing in common. It wasn't long before she understood the extent of his commitment—he was often gone several months out of the year, traveling to the ranches around the Rockies.

"It was his love and his passion, and we came to understand that that's what he did," Hagler says. "I always had a passion for horses, too, but not to the depth of this man."

When their first son, Lee, was thirty days old, his father had him sitting on a horse. He didn't wait even that long with the second son, Shawn. Their family vacations were horse shows, mainly those for their paint horses. They tried to go on a vacation to Mexico once, but Keith was obviously uncomfortable having to relax when there was still work to be done somewhere.

And there was always work to be done. The sun dictated his work days. When it was out, so was he.

"Even if he had all his work done, he'd be outside in the barn until sunset, looking for something to do," says Shawn. "His whole philosophy in life was his work ethic. He judged people on how hard they would work. He'd share his knowledge, but only if you were willing to work for it."

After a weekend at home, he would leave at four in the morning to get up to the ranch near Craig. That way he could still get there in time for a full day's work.

On the booklet for Hagler's funeral, they included "The Cowboy's Prayer." At the service they sang "Home on the Range." Afterwards, they put his body in an old horse-drawn carriage, with Shawn at the reins. Lee followed behind, on one of his father's horses named Trailer.

Behind them all walked Trucker, Keith Hagler's favorite horse. On his back sat a saddle that was in every way well worn.

For the first time in that horse's life, the boots in the stirrups were empty.

Eighty-five Years in Eighty-eight Keys

Marian Morrison Robinson

HER LIFE PLAYED OUT on the old piano. Eighty-five years in eighty-eight keys.

The Steinway first arrived when the little girl was seven years old, not long after she watched the Ku Klux Klan burn a cross in her family's front yard. A few years later, she saw Duke Ellington and Count Basie sit at the piano stool, where they composed songs with her father.

On the same keys, her tiny hands grew into the lithe, learned fingers of a woman, and eventually into the aged, accomplished hands of a historian, teacher, and leader.

"If only pianos could talk, the stories they could tell," said George Bailey, as he sat at his mother's grand piano in her Denver home.

"Actually," he said, lifting the worn wood, revealing the keys, "they do talk."

Marian Morrison Robinson died May 18, 2003, of complications following a stroke. She was eighty-five.

ON THE STEINWAY'S MUSIC STAND is a composition dedicated
to "Marian May and Junior Morrison," a piece called "Lullaby,"
written by Robinson's father, Denver jazz legend George Morrison
Sr. On the left margin of the piece is his instruction on how to play
the tune:

"With tenderness."

It's the way she was taught to play, her son says; it's the way
she tried to live.

The music began long before she was born, as her father
made a name for himself in jazz clubs around the country. Black
performers were not allowed to sleep in the hotels where they often
played, so many of them stayed at the Morrison home at 2558
Gilpin Street. There, the wide-eyed little girl watched them break in
her Steinway.

Marian graduated from Manual High School in 1935 and the
University of Denver in 1940. Near the same time her father was
turned down for the Denver Symphony Orchestra, she was denied
a teaching position in Denver because she was black.

It was nothing new. Despite family ties in the town dating back
to 1874, the family still had rocks thrown through their windows.

"She said, 'Not a day goes by that you're not reminded of
what color you are,'" her son said. "But she said, 'You have to take
the good and keep on going. It takes too much energy to get angry,
energy you could put into something positive.'"

Applying that philosophy, she started her career teaching
music in Missouri, then at a school for deaf and blind students

in Texas. In the 1950s she returned home and taught music in the Denver public schools for more than twenty years.

WHILE RAISING A FAMILY—she married twice—she kept a meticulous museum of Morrison family history. She also continued to play music, both professionally and at the Shorter AME Church.

"As an accompanist, the most important thing is not to dominate, not to overcome the soloist," said Bailey, who accompanies the Stuttgart Ballet Company in Germany. "She could play beautifully, but she was always in the background. She had such a soft touch."

As he sat at the old piano in her empty home, her son played the first notes of a song he wrote for the woman who first guided his hands over those same keys, the woman he always called "Honeybunch."

For the first time, he played the song without her.

My honeybunch, I love you
I'm sure you know that I do
For in my prayers God answers me
And I know that in His grace you will always be
My honeybunch. I love you.

Counting on Life's Tiniest Beads

Floy Box Valdez

HER BEADS ARE THE SIZE of flower seeds, sewn together in perfect patterns of reds, yellows, and blues, held tough through tragedy, held tight through tradition.

"She would bend over like this, looking down at her hands," Erwin Taylor says, as he hunches over into his mother's favorite position, stringing the tiny beads into the patterns she saw in her mind.

"She always wore a scarf over her head, an elaborate scarf. And she would start to sing. It was a traditional song that was often sung during the Sun Dance, but she sang it while she was beading."

As a little girl on the Southern Ute Reservation, Floy Box Valdez held close the traditions of her family; after she was left an orphan, the traditions were all she had.

After losing her parents, she would end up in a place where new teachers tried to take her language, and she would promise never to forget. As a young mother, she would lose two of her sons. She would lose her legs in a massive gas explosion that leveled her house, and she would raise her children alone. Then she would lose her eyesight.

Through it all, she continued to retreat to the tiny beads, leather, and thread, hunched over, quietly stringing the colors, providing their accompaniment.

"Her favorite was a Ute song, something you usually sing early in the day, but she sang it all the time. It was more or less like a healing song," Taylor says. "It was a song of being thankful, thankful for the new day."

Floy Box Valdez died January 26, 2002, in Ignacio. She was eighty.

INSIDE HER TINY HOME near Bayfield, eighty-three-year-old Ruby Garcia looks over at the cabinet where she keeps Valdez's beads, remembering the first time she heard about the pretty little girl that would become her stepsister.

"Her mother came to my mother and said, 'I know I'm dying, please take care of my daughter.' I remember when she first came here," Garcia says.

"She was a tough woman. Strong. Determined. If I was in her shoes, I think I would have died a long, long time ago."

Along with other Ute children, she was sent to a nearby government-run boarding school where the children hid their language in secret whispers.

"The teachers would always tell the children that they didn't want them to speak the native tongue," her son says. "When the children spoke anything but English they would lock them in a closet, and they would stay in there for hours."

After making it through the eighth grade, she later married one of her stepbrothers, who went to work in a steel mill in Pueblo. Meanwhile, Valdez stayed home with the five children in Ignacio. There, she taught her children to fish and the secrets of cooking her frybread and wild game stews. She took them to meet with elders of the tribe and had them learn their stories. She walked miles gathering herbs for traditional dances.

"She taught us to value where we came from and to remember who we are," says her daughter, EvaLee O'John Taylor. "She taught us not to forget our language and to keep our music."

In the 1950s she divorced, remarried, and had three more children. They were all in the house one morning in 1956 when Valdez walked into her kitchen to make breakfast, unaware of a gas leak in the basement of the house. She turned on the stove and the house exploded. Everyone was taken to the hospital, some with serious burn injuries. Valdez's legs were amputated below the knees. Her first request was to speak with her children.

"After the explosion, even though she had her legs cut off, she came and talked to us kids. She told us not to be afraid," Erwin Taylor says. "She told us that everything would be all right, and not to worry about the past, but to continue to work together."

ON PROSTHETIC LEGS, she rebuilt the family. Shortly after the house explosion she divorced again and spent the rest of her life with her children and grandchildren in Ignacio. After the deaths of two of her sons—one from accidental carbon monoxide poisoning, the other from a seizure disorder—she continued to draw strength from the tribe and joined its prestigious committee of elders.

"To me, she was a role model to most of the Indian women, young and old alike," says Pearl Casias, tribal counselor. "She was a great teacher when it came to traditions, to arts and crafts, but also as a grandmother, a friend, and a sister. She was not just there for the immediate family, but for her extended family, for the tribe, and anyone who wanted to learn from this great lady."

Valdez worked for the tribe in a beading co-op, creating belts, headbands, bracelets, purses, moccasins, shirts, and dresses. As she beaded, she taught the craft to the next generation.

"Now when I look at that work, that beautiful work, I realize how amazing it is," Taylor says. "It will hold tight for years and years."

Diabetes began a slew of health problems that soon multiplied. After she went blind in the mid-1990s, she was forced to use a wheelchair. Then her kidneys began to fail.

She probably could have lived longer, friends say, but that would have meant restricting her diet and her way of life. By then, she was long past the point where anyone could tell her how to live.

Recently, she called her friend Ruby Garcia and told her she was ready to die. She called her daughter and told her she was ready to take "another long journey."

"It was hard for her when she stopped beading, because that's what she loved to do, was to bead. But she had all those memories of those beads she made; she cherished them," Taylor says.

"She said, 'Even though you're blind, you can still see. You can see the memories.'"

The Leprechaun Who Shared His Treasure

Clarence Paul 'Clancy' Sheehy

THERE WAS SOMETHING THE CHILDREN saw in the breakable man with the wide blue eyes. There was something he saw in them.

When he was a child, some kids once tormented him because he was different. Later, it was children who taught him to read. When he was an adult, the children continued to gather around him, and this time he helped protect them. Then he taught them to sing.

"He always had a message to children, something that would teach a child something," says his sister, Beverly Brzezicki. "He loved children and they were fascinated with him."

Some adults called him the Boulder leprechaun, others knew him as the puppeteer or the tie-dye-wearing bookstore owner. He answered to all of those, but to the children, the four-foot-three-inch tall man would just wink and ask that they call him Clancy.

"I have a close relationship with children," Clancy Sheehy liked to say. "You could say we see eye to eye."

Clarence Paul Sheehy died December 11, 2000. He was seventy-three.

HIS FIRST BONE BROKE when baby Sheehy was three months old. Thirty-nine more would break by the time he was fourteen. Long before doctors diagnosed him with osteogenesis imperfecta—also known as brittle bone disease—his parents were carrying him around the house on a pillow.

"I remember that before we had a wheelchair we'd pull him around in a little red wagon. I remember he was just so breakable," says Brzezicki, who remained his best friend throughout his life. She recalls taking him to the movies in Denver, where he broke his leg lifting it up for someone to pass by.

"He never cried," she says. "I was the one who would always cry, and he was the one who would comfort me."

During an interview in 1997, Sheehy recalled a time as a child when he was left alone in the wagon, and school kids surrounded him, hurling taunts.

"When I think of this event, I can still feel in me the hurt and frightened sensation in the pit of my stomach," he remembered. "At that point, I didn't know I looked different than any other children—my family always made me feel more special than different."

As the eight-year-olds picked on him, he thought back to the songs his father sang on the banjo and saved himself the only way he knew how.

"I instinctively began to sing funny songs like 'You Are My Sunshine' and 'The Sunny Side of the Street,' and some of the kids even sang along," he said. "That's when I realized I could take my disability and turn it into an advantage."

Because he couldn't attend public school, Sheehy's sister taught him to read using her *Run Spot Run* books, and a friend showed him other stories. He was soon onto *The Yearling,* then in love with *Gone With the Wind.* When the Boettcher School for Handicapped Children opened, he was one of the first in line, and graduated at the age of twenty-one.

By then he had taken a few trips to Boulder, and he knew where he was headed next. By then he had seen the inside of the University of Colorado's Norlin Library.

First, however, his sister would finally see him cry.

IN 1955, SHEEHY'S RIGHT LEG was amputated due to numerous fractures that twisted it, leaving it useless. Afterward, his sister saw the tears.

"He had these phantom pains—it felt like he still had his leg and someone was twisting his foot," she says. "The first time he walked, it took him four hours to walk half a block. But he did it."

On his own for the first time—walking with the aid of crutches and a prosthetic leg—he headed for Boulder and graduated from CU with a degree in English literature. Yearning for more books, he started his own shop on University Hill and called it Clancy's Upstairs Bookstore. He was soon attracting the likes of poet Allen Ginsberg and LSD advocate Timothy Leary, who invited him to help stage a "be-in."

In 1966, a policeman walked into the store and saw a collection of lapel buttons for sale—buttons with liberal slogans of the time such as "conserve water, shower with a friend." Ironically, the one that got Sheehy in trouble was one that said "F--- Censorship."

Though Sheehy was charged with selling indecent material, the immediate uproar from friends, college professors—and even local clergy—throughout the town quickly forced the city government to drop the charges and squash the obscenity law.

In 1968, at the age of forty-one, he closed the bookstore and headed for San Francisco, where despite his still-fragile frame he participated in some of the country's most heated debates and demonstrations over the Vietnam War, before returning to Boulder in 1971.

"I always said I was one of the oldest and shortest hippies," Sheehy said.

MANY OF THE PEOPLE at Clancy Sheehy's memorial service first met him eye to eye at one of the thousands of puppet shows he presented to children across Colorado during the past thirty years. After learning to make the puppets, Sheehy performed wherever he could—on the Pearl Street Mall, in festivals, and birthday parties. He even traveled to schools to teach children to create their own puppets. Then, with his rich history of Irish legends and grasp of fine literature, he would begin to weave stories.

"When he started being a puppeteer he could just see the magic on these children's faces, how they could relate to these puppets," his sister says. "And every puppet show had to teach a lesson."

He continued to teach those lessons as a board member of the Parenting Place, a center in Boulder designed to help young mothers and children. He volunteered to help in gerontology classes at the Buddhist-affiliated Naropa University, and students studying the aging process would interview him about his philosophy of growing old.

As a thank you, one of the students paid his way to Ireland.

"I wanted to kiss the Blarney stone—not that I needed it," he once said, referring to the stone's purported gift of eloquence. "I climbed 169 steps to kiss the Blarney, and a bunch of old ladies said they'd rather kiss me than the stone."

Parenting Place founder Dr. Bob McFarland has another image of his friend's trip to Ireland.

"Clancy climbed up all those steps to kiss the Blarney stone," McFarland says. "When he was finished, the Blarney stone said, 'Thank you, Clancy.'"

At the memorial service, friends remembered watching him at Boulder Reservoir, where he would take off his prosthetic leg, crawl into the water, and float like a beach ball. They played a tape of him talking and singing. As usual, Sheehy set the stage.

"We're sitting under a juniper tree and the skies are blue," he said on the tape, then asked, "What's the best way to lie?

"On your back and looking at the sky."

THEN THERE'S THE STORY of the leprechaun.

"It started when he was up in Maine, sitting under a tree reading when these teenagers found him," his sister says.

The teenagers told him he was in their secret cigarette smoking spot and began asking him who he was, what he was doing there.

"They were surprised to see this little man sitting under this tree," Brzezicki says. "One of them said, 'Are you a leprechaun? Where's the gold? Where's the gold?'"

Sheehy was so taken with the notion that he began dressing as a leprechaun for countless St. Patrick's Day parades, wearing an outfit stitched by his sister. He continued the tradition until 1996, when his health finally kept him from participating. He eventually moved in with Brzezicki in Denver, then into an assisted living facility, but she still tucked him in nearly every night.

And that pot of gold? Unlike most leprechauns, Sheehy would gladly lead anyone straight to it.

"You can only find the real pot of gold when you're with your friends, doing good things in life," he said.

"I like to tell the children that the real pot of gold is in your heart. That's how we keep it alive."

Choosing the Last Letters

Marie Coombs

INSIDE A BUILDING THE COLOR of old newsprint, Dean Coombs sits at an enormous black eighty-year-old machine, slowly typing the next week's newspaper, letter by letter.

"If you get in a hurry, it doesn't seem to be advantageous," he says. "The letters don't fall right. I can always tell when I start going too fast because it starts acting up."

For nearly eighty years this was his mother's job, working at the old Linotype machine. These days, the *Saguache Crescent* is one of only about five newspapers in the country that still uses the Linotypes, which cast the letters, line by line, out of molten metal.

As Coombs types the letters, the machine whirrs in the background. The letters zip around the contraption, making a racket that sounds like someone throwing nickels at a tin roof. It could break down any minute, Coombs says. Then it does.

"You know, it becomes like a relative. It has a personality," Coombs says as he adjusts one of the belts and clears a bunch of letter Ts that have fallen through a crack. "Sometimes it gives you a lot of trouble and you can't do anything right."

A few weeks ago he sat here, alone, trying to figure out what to say about the woman who always seemed to get along with the machine.

"I had to write the story. I'm the only one here, so I'm the only one who could write it," he says. "But since I don't write a lot of things, it was kind of hard to figure out where to begin and where to end."

He pulls out a newspaper and points to the front page.

"Marie Coombs, long-time editor of the *Saguache Crescent*, died Monday, March 25, 2002, at the age of 87."

"I started writing her obituary," he says. "And you know what? The machine gave me no trouble at all."

THE OLD LINOTYPE was manufactured in 1921, when Marie was six years old. By then she had already worked at the newspaper for two years. Her father, Charles Ogden, bought the paper in 1917, and Marie grew up among the presses, along with her older sister, Irene.

She attended school in Saguache in the San Luis Valley but found more important lessons at the newspaper, where she learned to set type by hand and to master the Linotype. When her father died in 1935, her mother named her editor of the paper, and she held the title pretty much ever since.

The two sisters married in a double wedding in 1938, and the family continued to run the paper, with Marie's husband Ivan serving as publisher until his death of a sudden heart attack the day after Christmas in 1978.

"At that point we were either in or out, and in a crisis you do the things that you know, so we kept it going," says Dean Coombs, who started working at the paper as a young boy and has toiled for sixty-hour weeks as publisher since his father's death.

From Marie's familiar place at the front of the shop she often held court while clacking away at the Linotype. She was a great speller and proofer but otherwise disorganized, somewhat eccentric, and a notorious packrat—still evident by the thousands of yellowing newspaper pages stacked around the office. She was a perfectionist with an ever-changing concept of perfection, and plenty of arguments began and finished among the din of the presses.

But there was one tenet that never wavered: the mandate to print the good news. A typical four-page edition of the *Crescent* is filled with amateur poetry, upcoming birthdays of local residents, and words of wisdom from historical figures. When the paper went to press the week of September 11, 2001, there was no mention of the terrorist attacks. Next to his mother's obituary on March 28, Dean ran a story about a Saguache youngster who won a local Lego contest.

"I've had people tell me this is the only newspaper they can read and still sleep at night," she once told a reporter.

As the editions piled up over the years, Marie Coombs looked like a little old lady long before she was one. At just under five feet tall, she ate like a sparrow and appeared especially fragile next to the gigantic manual presses. In private, she didn't waver much from her public persona. Her diaries are full of mundane information about life in the area: the weather, the people she met—the same information found in the *Crescent*.

As community newspapers around the country switched to
modern printing methods, she and her son refused to change. Not
a single computer sits in the offices of the paper; in a bind, Dean
Coombs could put the whole thing out by wind or water power. For
the bulk of her life, Marie was just as dependable. In the past year,
her health began to fail, but Dean would still bring her papers to
fold even after she moved to a nearby nursing home.

"Most of these little newspapers (around the country) just
wore out. The machines wore out. The people wore out," he says.
"She was very, very ... durable."

ABOVE THE METAL JIGSAW-PUZZLE layout of next week's paper,
Dean Coombs looks through a few of the lead lines he's saved over
the years and finds the most recent: "Marie Coombs, editor," he
says, reading the chunk of type.

*"It was strange to pull the slug with Marie's name on it from
the masthead of the*

Pillows in
Grandpa's Tractor

Albert 'Fritz' Albrandt

IN DOWNTOWN MERINO, the shop windows have long been replaced by plywood, but there are still plenty of people who can see beyond the boards.

"That used to be a bank. That used to be a creamery. That used to be a grocery store," says Alan Albrandt, as he eases his car down the empty main street. "That was the filling station. There used to be three filling stations here."

These days, there are no gas stations or grocery stores in Merino. The only business on the downtown strip is Mom's Cafe, where the talk in the morning has never changed: tractors and heifers, sugar beets and corn.

These days, something else is missing in the tiny northeastern Colorado town—a man who lived his entire life within a couple miles of here, raising tons of crops and years of spirits.

"I remember when a farmer nearby won the lottery of a million dollars," says Alan, son of "Fritz" Albrandt. "Someone asked, 'Hey, Fritz, what would you do if you won the lottery?' and he said, 'I'd probably farm until it was all gone. That might take three or four years.'"

When they tell that story today, the men from the breakfast club laugh again, then stare into their coffee mugs.

Albert "Fritz" Albrandt died January 5, 2000. He was seventy-nine.

ON A CORNER OF THE ALBRANDT FARM, Alan hops over a few strands of barbed wire and walks over to a historic marker proclaiming the site of the area's first school.

"Jimmy Chambers, first permanent settler in the South Platte in 1872 ... gave one acre for a school in the first school district of what was to be Logan County."

Albert Albrandt's parents arrived about fifty years after Jimmy Chambers, settling on the plains near the river. The German farmers had been moved to Russia by Catherine the Great, and to the United States by tales of soil even more fertile.

Albert was born in 1920, the year the family came to an area about a dozen miles southwest of Sterling. Seven years later, his father was killed in a farm accident, leaving the youngster, along with his older sisters, to band together with their mother to keep the farm alive.

Today, two giant wooden letter 'A's dominate the Albrandt barn, one atop another, in a brand that has lasted decades. Surrounding the house is the land where Albrandt knew the furrows in the ground as well as those on his skin—a place where he saw the sunrise pour across the fields each day of his life.

"He never, ever considered leaving the farm, even when times were bad," says his son, Randal. "He never even discussed it."

ONE OF THE FIRST TIMES Helen Hettinger heard Albert Albrandt, the boy was barking underneath her window.

"Yes, barking," laughs the woman he married in 1943. "He was underneath the school window, trying to get my attention."

It was one of the many ways Albert was known to make people smile—whether it was his endless supply of jokes, his storytelling expertise, or his ability to play the harmonica with his nose.

As he drove around town and the fields, Albrandt brought his own soundtrack along—the polka tunes he grew up with, the music he and his wife would dance to at socials across the state.

"One night in Sterling they put a meter on him—he danced thirteen miles that night. He would just dance. Such great fun. It's a great way to keep young," Helen Albrandt says and then smiles. "You know how it does you good to just laugh so hard," she says. "We had a lot of those times."

ON THE ALBRANDT FARM, the smiles were tempered with work.

"Back then, nobody was fat, and nobody jogged," Helen says. "We worked, and it was good for us. At the time we didn't think it was but it was. There was no word in our dictionary for 'jog.'"

For his efforts, Fritz Albrandt was named ten times as one of Logan County's "High Ten"—the prestigious designation for the top sugar beet growers. He served on several farm organizations and emceed events throughout the region, peppering his speeches with his trademark wit.

Even as he passed seventy, he continued to work on the farm and raise cattle with his son Darrell. Though his sons Alan and Randal moved to the Denver area, they continued to return with their children, where "Grandpa" Fritz introduced them to the soil.

On the floor of the tractor, he piled pillows and work clothes, so that when the children got tired, they could fall asleep in the cab of the massive machine. His grandson Lance's first word was "tractor."

In the evening, the old man was known to take the kids over to a nearby plant that manufactured carnival rides after the workers had left for the day. As the children sat on the silent rides surrounded by farmland, he would pretend to bring the machines to life.

"The most important thing in our lives is family. It's family," Helen Albrandt says. "We're so proud."

She remembers her husband drifting into a coma during his last days of life, and one of the last things he said: "Good boys, good boys."

INSIDE DARRELL'S HOME on the family farm, the Albrandts gather around the table, hold hands, and say grace. It's something Fritz Albrandt did every day.

"Just recently, he said, 'You know, we've had such a good life. We haven't had many problems, we have a wonderful family, and we've done just fine,'" Helen says. "'We aren't rich, but money don't buy happiness.'"

As dinner begins, she remembers a story her husband told of the priest asking him what he prayed for at church.

"'I can't think of anything to pray for,' he said. 'I'm too busy thanking God for what I have.'"

After 624 Deaths, One More

Carolyn Jaffe

THE MAN LAY ON THE COUCH, waiting for the tiny, white-haired woman who would appear whenever he needed her, throughout the last months of his life.

Before saying a word, Carolyn Jaffe walked to the patient and dropped to her knees.

"It was so symbolic and so appropriate," said Janelle McCallum-Orozco, a nurse who once accompanied Jaffe to her patients' homes. "We talked about it later and she said 'That's the most important thing. You should never stand over someone. You should get down to their level.'

"She would get in their space, in their feeling, and willingly get into their place of pain."

It was a scene that nurse Jaffe repeated 624 times, for each of the terminally ill patients she would care for in more than twenty years, in her commitment until the final breath.

People often ask me how I could stand it all these years, taking on one patient after another knowing they all would die; saying goodbye over and over—as one life after another ended, Jaffe once wrote. *It is true—I lose a friend when a patient dies, sometimes a dear friend. I hurt when I say goodbye. Often I cry. But then I turn around and take another family, another patient. I do so because I feel sure and strong about what I do; it's so right. I feel rich. I've been rewarded.*

As the cofounder of Hospice of Metro Denver, she made it possible for thousands of terminally ill patients to die peacefully at home, surrounded by family instead of strangers. As a nurse, she never allowed herself to forget the power and poignancy of every life, and would share the lessons that come from listening to last words.

"Carolyn does something to you. I think of death differently. I think of life differently," said Bev Sloan, director of Hospice of Metro Denver. "We always say that hospice work is the work of angels," Sloan said. "And she was our first and foremost angel."

Carolyn Jaffe died September 27, 2001. She was seventy-six.

THE FIRST PERSON CAROLYN EVER SAW—the nurse who brought her into the world—would have the greatest impact on her life.

The fifth child in a family struggling through the Depression in Youngstown, Ohio, Carolyn's crib was a drawer pulled out of a dresser. As the only Jewish family in a poor Catholic neighborhood, tough times were made even tougher. As a child, Carolyn made friends with three neighbors, two of whom were nurses. As she grew older, she visited their home at every opportunity, learning about their lives and profession. When the nurse who had birthed

Carolyn had a stroke, the young girl went to visit the woman in the hospital.

"She was in a coma and I could see nasty bedsores on her heels and elbows from lying for hours in the same position," she later wrote. *"The sight of those raw ulcers made me sick to my stomach. Then I got angry. How could anyone in a hospital care so poorly for my dear Helen?*

"I knew then that I would become a nurse. I don't believe I made a deliberate decision—I just knew. I would become a super-nurse."

She graduated from nursing school in 1946 and began work in a local emergency room, where she met a young intern named Marvin Jaffe. After their marriage, the couple worked together in veterans' hospitals for several years, then moved to Denver in 1957 with their daughter and son.

While she worked as a nurse in the intensive care unit, memories of her old friend Helen resurfaced. As in most hospitals at the time, death was seen as failure, even in terminally ill patients, and dying people with no chance of recovery were often hooked to machines, continually resuscitated as doctors attempted to stave off the inevitable.

At the same time, a new idea was spreading through the country, a philosophy to make dying patients as comfortable as possible, to mitigate their pain, and to prepare the patients and their families for death. With help from other burgeoning hospice organizations and a small grant from the American Cancer Society, Jaffe helmed Hospice of Metro Denver, which in its first year cared for about twenty patients. Since then, more than 35,000 patients and their families have experienced her vision.

"The word that comes to mind is beauty, and that's a word that's easy to use in a place like Colorado," said Ken Fish, whose wife was cared for by Jaffe. "If you've been to the top of a mountain and looked out at the panoramic vista that's there, you've seen beauty. If, on a fall day, you've watched as the sunrise starts to reflect on the east side of the Denver skyline while at the same time a full moon is setting over the mountains, you've seen beauty. But until you are in the position of dealing with life-threatening illness ... and it's four in the morning and something unusual and unexpected happens and you're scared, and you place a call, and within minutes on your front porch is Carolyn Jaffe in her running shoes and sweats—until you've experienced that, you don't have a clue of what true beauty is."

After entering a patient's home, she would often cook, clean, and talk to family members as if they were her own. Some of those family members became her best friends; others became dedicated hospice volunteers.

In 1990, Jaffe received the prestigious Nightingale Award, one of the highest honors in nursing. In 1995, the University of Denver recognized her with an honorary doctorate of humane letters. Despite the accolades, she remained grounded and self-deprecating, sharing her mistakes to help others learn.

In 1997, she wrote a book with her friend Carol Ehrlich. Taken mainly from taped conversations with Jaffe, the book details her experiences as a hospice nurse. Its title reflects her philosophy: *"All Kinds of Love."*

DYING IS NEVER EASY, she wrote. *Suffering and grief are always part of dying. But closeness and warmth can be there, too. If I've done my job well, I feel the warmth and the closeness. I share the laughter and love. I know I've made the time better. I've changed the dying from something that's feared, something that's the enemy, to a natural part of life—maybe even a friend. The families tell me this, and I know it without their saying a word. This is powerful; it is beautiful.*

Carolyn Jaffe didn't die at home. Still, coworkers say, hers was a hospice death.

In September a heart problem sent her to the hospital and doctors scheduled surgery, then decided that her weakened body couldn't take the stress. Before she could be sent home, she had another heart attack and was given only hours to live.

Her daughter, Mindy Jaffe, was already on a plane from Hawaii, where she served as a state representative. Her son, Evan Jaffe, was on his way from New Jersey, where he is a rabbi. Carolyn Jaffe allowed doctors to use a respirator to keep her alive for the few hours it took for her children to arrive. As she raced to the hospital, Mindy thought back to all her mother had taught and wondered what she was about to see.

"I didn't know how I would react. I've never been to a funeral. I've never seen a dead person before," Mindy said. "But we weren't afraid. I somehow knew it was nothing to fear. We were real prepared because we had talked about it for thirty years."

Once the family finally made it to her hospital room, Carolyn Jaffe scribbled on a note that it was time for her to go. When the tube was removed, her life would last about forty minutes.

As the little white-haired lady drifted away, her husband and children gathered around and held her hands. Her daughter bent down to her, on her level, just as her mother had taught.

"As she was taking her last breaths, I got up next to her and breathed in the air as she breathed it out," Mindy Jaffe said. "She gave me my first breath, and I was taking in her last.

"For me, it was a passing of the torch. I felt very comfortable, right there, breathing in my mother's last breaths. It seemed like the most natural thing in the world.

"It was a lovely goodbye."

Mr. Colorado's Weakness

Ray McGuire

THE OLD BIKES ARE STILL ON RAY MCGUIRE'S front porch.
Some are caked with rust, others missing more parts than they
have, but there they wait, brought home by the man who knew
potential when he saw it.

"The first bike he got had garden hose for tires," says his wife,
Dorothy McGuire. "He was about nine years old, and that was all
he could afford."

Back in the 1930s, the scraggly, scrawny short kid and the
beaten-down bike seemed the perfect match. As it turned out, they
were.

After some hard work, young Ray replaced the hoses with real
tires. He got a paper route, and, with the money he earned, he and
the bike fixed each other up.

He never gave up on much at all after that.

Ray McGuire died March 4, 2001, of prostate cancer. He was seventy-one.

HE GREW UP IN A SMALL HOME in north Denver—a home long since bulldozed over. They called him the ninety-eight-pound weakling, but that wasn't true; when he entered North High School, he actually weighed 103 pounds. After high school he was headed in whichever direction his motorcycle took him. The Korean War changed all that.

He hoped to travel with the Air Force but never got farther than Cheyenne, as a supply sergeant stationed stateside. During his service a motorcycle crash left him with more than a hundred stitches in his head, forming a scar that ran the length of his black flattop.

After his recovery, McGuire began lifting weights. Within weeks he was lifting at every chance, competing in bodybuilding contests. Soon the once-scrawny, five-foot-eight soldier was considered "essential personnel" and was put on patrol to help find cadets gone AWOL. When soldiers saw the menacing tree trunk of a man coming for them, nobody ran.

After his service, McGuire went back home. Nobody in his family had attended college before him, and nobody expected anything else from him. Still, he threw some clothes in a grocery bag and, thanks to the GI bill, headed for Fort Collins.

After starting at Colorado State University, Ray was recruited to the University of Northern Colorado by the wrestling coach. He won the title for his weight class four years straight, and in 1956 he was named "Mr. Colorado," winning not only the overall bodybuilding trophy but also the top ranking in every individual muscle group.

Long before graduation, he knew exactly what he wanted to do and where he wanted to do it.

FOR BOYS ENTERING THE GYM at Aurora Central High School, the first image was a lasting one.

"I remember the first time I saw him I was scared to death. It was like seeing Zeus," said Craig Truman, now a well-known attorney in Denver and one of the thousands of boys who called McGuire "Coach" from 1959 until 1989.

As the boys came in for physical education class, McGuire recognized many of them before he met them.

"A lot of kids at Aurora Central had no motivation to be anything than what they had been. These were kids that nobody thought anything good would come out of," his wife says. "He would see these kids with every strike against them. Emotionally, he knew how that felt. And it just tore him up."

McGuire's father had never attended a single wrestling match or bodybuilding competition to watch his son. For some of the kids at Aurora Central, McGuire filled in for the man who was never there.

In his gym class, former students say, he wasn't one to throw out the footballs and let the kids fend for themselves. Instead, he involved everyone.

"You're always going to have kids who were overweight and uncoordinated," says Terry Truman , who also had McGuire as a coach. "If you were one of those kids, you could get extra credit if you went into his office and said vocabulary words. So the kids who were brainy and not athletic didn't have to say goodbye to their P.E. grade."

That didn't mean McGuire was a pushover. If he caught someone being truant, he'd make them do the "dirty ten," which consisted of one hundred sit-ups, one hundred pushups, and eight other grueling exercises. Kids who skipped school, it was said, would still come to P.E.

In the summers McGuire taught tennis and handball for the City of Aurora, then in the afternoons he would teach tennis in Cherry Creek. All his spare money went to keep a promise that the family would never be in debt.

At Cherry Creek Presbyterian Church, McGuire also stood out—not only for his physical presence but for his penchant for belting out hymns at the top of his lungs, regardless of his ability to carry a note. Enthusiasm made up for his lack of pitch, however, and he helped teach Sunday school for years.

After he retired, McGuire continued to referee wrestling matches until he was seventy—a total of thirty-nine years as a referee. Though he kept himself in top shape, none of his new friends knew of his prestigious past.

"He never allowed me to tell anybody he was Mr. Colorado. He never allowed me to put out his trophies," Dorothy McGuire says.

Instead, Ray McGuire was the one handing out trophies of his own, such as the one he made for Don Robinson, whom he grew up with and later taught alongside at Aurora Central. Robinson later taught gymnastics at Arizona State.

"I had Olympians on my team. I've been around the world because of gymnastics, but I always thought it should be Ray," instead of him, says Robinson. "My most precious trophy was from him, a brass eagle that Ray made for me. I couldn't have possibly won the accolades or awards I did if it weren't for his influence. That period of time was a mold set for me by him. He was a champion all the way."

Robinson was one of the hundreds of people who visited McGuire in his last days.

"At the hospital, one of the nurses finally asked, 'Who is he?' thinking that to have all these visitors, he must be somebody important," his wife says. "Well, he was important to a lot of kids."

THE MCGUIRE GARAGE is a tornado's aftermath of bicycle parts scattered across the floor. Boxes filled with pedals spill into rusty clumps of chains and bony aluminum frames.

"He fixed thousands, and he did it for so many years. Every spring he would start buying bikes, and during the summer he would fix them," his wife says. "He was one of the best bike fixers around, because he had seen the evolution of the bicycles, from the old one-speeds to these road racers.

"He couldn't stand to see a bicycle with some hope just sitting near a trash can," she says.

Many kids in Denver grew up riding on McGuire bikes brought to life by the man who once rode on garden hoses.

"If a kid said he couldn't afford it he'd say, 'Come over and mow my lawn for a couple weeks and I'll give you the bike,'" Dorothy McGuire says. "A lot of people got on him for giving so much away."

When he wasn't fixing bicycles or working out, McGuire was likely digging in the dirt around the state, looking to add to his arrowhead collection, or digging through piles of junk at flea markets and garage sales, looking for stuff nobody wanted.

Inside a display case in their living room are lead soldiers, a collection of old bicycle license plates, and a knob from a Model A stick shift. There are dozens of tarnished pocket watches and an old thermometer he just plain thought was neat. There are a historical collection of barbed wire and thirty pairs of cowboy boots—one for every day of the month.

On her back porch, Dorothy McGuire walks over to one of the old bicycles and takes hold of a handlebar.

"There are all these things that he found. He was just interested in things," his wife says. "And how things changed."

Lessons From
an Imperfect Teacher

Dan Sarlo

THEY STILL TALK ABOUT HIM like he was perfect, which isn't that uncommon after someone dies.

No, they say, this time they really, really mean it. Because now they know he wasn't perfect at all.

"We would all like to think that we're accepting of other people, but he was the most accepting person I ever knew," says his former coach and later friend, Kelly Meek. "He was the most gifted leader I've ever seen."

"Right away I could tell how much he cared about other people, and how he had devoted his life to helping others," says his friend Renee Dupont. "He was just the kindest and most gentle man I've ever met."

"He was very giving, very kind," says Malcolm Moore, the girls' basketball coach at ThunderRidge High School in Highlands Ranch. "People just say that, but this is for real."

In the classroom, Dan Sarlo was known for his ability to captivate the toughest of audiences. He was among the smartest teachers in any school where he taught—and the least intimidating. Away from the classroom, he inspired kids on the basketball court, and in the Peace Corps he did the same on a new playing field.

"I don't know how many times I told him 'If I was to pick a perfect person, it was you,'" Meek says, and then he pauses.

"I wish I could go back in time and pull those words back. To lay that on someone. ...We made him out to be like a god that walks among us, and that's not human life."

Dan Sarlo died September 16, 2000, in Denver. He was forty.

"The only bad thing I can say about Dan," his mother says, "is that he didn't let us help him."

HIS ENTIRE LIFE, DANNY SARLO excelled in school. As a child, he read constantly, breezing through early grades. At Regis Jesuit High School in Denver and later at Steamboat Springs High School, he maintained a 4.0 average and was named a Boettcher scholar. He was class president and played on the all-state basketball team.

With his grades he could have gone most anywhere. Using the benefits of his scholarship, he headed to Colorado College with plans to teach.

"At the time there was a teachers glut. They said, 'Well, they have a lot of teachers,'" his mother remembers. "I said, 'Well they don't have a Danny.'"

He started where he found his first true mentors, at Regis, and in the late eighties he was named teacher of the year, and the yearbook was dedicated to him. Teachers and students compare Sarlo to the Robin Williams character in the film *Dead Poet's*

Society. They talk about him jumping on desks, flailing around the room, and encouraging his students to do the same. They talk about him pushing the imaginary boundaries of the classroom and the limits of personal accomplishment on the playing field.

"To me he was like the moisture that prepares the soil. He could permeate right into you and help you grow," says Meek, who coached Sarlo in Steamboat and later called him a friend. "He could pick me up when I was feeling down, and I was the one that was supposed to be motivating him. He got you to motivate yourself.

"I say you can read a person by the look in their eye, and the look in his eye. ... He was totally in tune with you and that what you had to say was so valuable."

After teaching at Regis for seven years, Sarlo left to join the Peace Corps. He was sent to Slovakia, where he taught English for four years. When he returned to Denver, he taught and coached at Gateway Senior High School in Aurora and then at ThunderRidge, where he helped start a program catering to at-risk kids.

"Dan made us realize how important kids are. Teaching was so important to him that other things became irrelevant," says Jerry Rouse, who attended Regis with Dan and later taught alongside him at ThunderRidge. "To be a teacher you redefine it in light of Dan, and that's a really good thing."

Friends say Sarlo was always concerned about underprivileged people, but after returning from Eastern Europe his interest intensified. He shunned materialism, shopping at thrift shops while donating most of his time and money to others; his mother referred to his apartment as "the hovel."

"He was always doing for us and other people, and we never did for Dan," Meek says. "Now we all wish we would have done something for Dan. We just figured he didn't need anything. But he did."

In August, Dan called his mother, asking her to take him to the hospital, saying he was in pain and couldn't drive himself. As they sat in the parking lot, he looked over at her.

"Mom," he said. "I think I'm an alcoholic."

BY THE TIME HE ENTERED the hospital, Dan Sarlo's liver was already shutting down.

Anyone calling his answering machine would have heard his cheerful voice recorded with his trademark dry humor: "Sorry I'm not home, I'm out waiting for Godot," a reference to Samuel Beckett's play. "I'll call you back when he returns."

A liver condition was intensified by his hidden addiction, his mother says. He spent three weeks in intensive care, but by then he had kept things to himself too long.

He had a spotless attendance record at school, his friends say—he taught and coached two days before entering the hospital. He never slipped up, they say, and then before you can ask his friends, "How could you not have known?" they're already asking themselves.

"I never said, 'Dan, is there something you need to talk about?' I never said it, because he ... because he was Dan," Meek says, remembering their last telephone conversation, which he now thinks ended awkwardly. "I'll betcha he was ready to break (during the call)—that he was ready to say 'I've got a problem,' but he didn't. He knew how to help others but he didn't know how to help himself."

When the school asked what teachers should tell the students, his mother didn't hesitate.

"Tell them the truth," she said.

"I want them to know that alcohol is a part of his death. I want them to know that it's an illness. He never lied in his life, and I'm not going to make his death a lie," she says. "I think he hid it because he was always told by teachers and coaches that he was perfect, and I think it's hard to live up to that."

Cheating Death Together

Harold and Catherine Helgoth

WHEN THE MAN ARRIVED AT THE doctor's office with a three-day-old rattlesnake fang in his leg, the doctor told him it was too late. It wasn't the first time Harold Helgoth should have died.

"He asked the doctor what he could do and the doctor said, 'Well, nothing. You survived it,'" says his son, Dick Helgoth, as he looks at a photo of his father posing next to a box of rattlesnake rattles. "There were two more times he was working and got bit by rattlers. He never went to the doctor, then, either. He figured if you survive it once, you're immune."

Those might have been his second and third lives. Or maybe his seventh and eighth. His wife, Catherine, said he must have nine, but he didn't seem to keep track of them.

When something like the rattlesnake bite happened, Catherine told her husband he should go to the doctor, and he knew that's what she would say. He figured the doctor's diagnosis proved him right. She figured the doctor proved her right. That would go back and forth for a while. It was a typical conversation between the two of them.

Harold never seemed to see the danger. There was the time a car slipped off a jack and onto his face. Then there was the time the plane he was flying nearly crashed, but he pulled out fifty feet above the ground.

As she toiled in the kitchen while caring for ten children, Catherine always managed to keep track of Harold, whether he was on the farm, in the air, or on the machines. She quietly worried about him, and he about her.

After all, she always thought she would be the one to die young.

"They were hardy people. Very resilient. And inspirational," says daughter Mary Noonan.

Noonan looks at her parents' wedding picture, that photo of the rattlesnake rattles, and another one of her father in his plane.

"I think he was such a risk-taker," she says. "Because he knew she would always be there."

Harold Nicholas Helgoth died September 23, 1999, in Boulder. He was eighty-eight. Catherine Anna Helgoth died thirty-one days later. She was eighty-three.

THE TWO FARMS WERE THREE MILES apart; the closest town was Fleming. The closest town most people knew of was Sterling.

Inside the one-room schoolhouse, the Helgoth boy was known to let loose a sackful of gophers every once in a while to hear the girls squeal, or hook a line of kids up to a car spark plug so they could feel the electricity. Catherine Brekel, his neighbor, was a few grades behind him, so she sat on the other side of the room, but she never lost track of him.

When Catherine was five years old, she survived a bout with diphtheria that everyone expected would kill her. When she was twelve, her mother died during childbirth at the age of thirty-eight. After that, Catherine always figured she would never make it past thirty-eight.

Along with her older sister and brother, Catherine took care of the other five children while their father worked. Next door, a few miles away, Harold Helgoth had been farming wheat since he was eleven. The children dreamed of the days they could make the trip to Sterling for an ice cream cone.

Once the two neighbors were old enough for the weekly barn dance, the nation had entered the Great Depression. About the same time, Harold got up the nerve to ask Catherine out.

For two weeks in a row they found each other at the dance. They married two years later, April 29, 1936.

They honeymooned in Denver, where Catherine was amazed by the streetcars.

THE FAMILY ISN'T EXACTLY SURE when Harold got the plane, but they have a newspaper article saying he had the first non-commercial pilot's license in Colorado.

As that story goes, he traded a car he had fixed up for the Piper Cub and learned to fly mostly by teaching himself.

"Ohhh, that flying," Noonan says. "He got tremendous enjoyment out of flying. Every time he'd talk about it his eyes would just light up."

During the early 1940s, the family moved to Holyoke and bought a 3,000-acre farm, meaning more work for everyone. About that time, he bought himself a violin and taught himself to play. When he found spare time, Harold found ways to share his passion for the plane.

"Dad tells this story about a doctor in Holyoke who he always wanted to go up with him, but the doctor said, 'No, my feet will never leave the ground,'" Dick Helgoth says.

"This one time the doctor came out to the house and dad said, 'C'mere, Doc, I want to show you something.' Dad had a bucket of dirt on the floor of the plane. Dad said, 'Sit here in this plane and put your feet in the bucket.'"

Technically, the doctor's feet never left the ground.

"That doctor enjoyed it so much he went again," Dick says.

Harold flew until 1949, when he got frustrated with the increase in air traffic. That and the fact that the government wouldn't let him deduct his flying expenses.

He never flew in a commercial aircraft. Didn't trust 'em.

THREE BEDROOMS, ONE BATHROOM, and twelve people.

"That old house is still there," son Jim Helgoth says of the home on 47th Street in Boulder. "It survived us."

The family had to move to the house in Boulder in 1947, after two of the children were diagnosed with severe asthma that made farm life impossible. It wasn't long before they settled into the small city.

Every Sunday at 6 a.m., the kids knew where they would be: filing into church, where six boys, four girls, and their parents took up an entire pew. The kids took care of each other while Harold went to work on a new farm he bought in Fort Lupton. At night, the children would fall asleep to the sounds of playing cards, their parents winding down, chiding each other on who had the better hand.

Looking for work during the winter, Harold opened an auto salvage yard. The business—later run by sons Dick and Doug Helgoth—was sold to the City of Boulder and is now a park. It was the last junkyard left in the town.

"Looking back," Dick Helgoth says, "he realized he should have gone into the real estate business."

HAROLD'S HANDS WERE STAINED by the grease of farm equipment and decades of dirt.

Catherine's hands were marked by the nicks of kitchen knives, from the thousands of apples she picked, peeled, and cooked in an effort to hold the family together with food.

The family had a large apple orchard in an area of Boulder now covered with homes and offices. The kids would help peel the apples and pull out the worms (the couple didn't believe in spraying for pests).

"Mom had so many things to do with apples. Applesauce cake, pie, strudel. She'd bake five apple pies at a time, and two days later all the boys had eaten them, so she baked five more. She'd have cinnamon rolls waiting for us when we got home from school, and they'd be gone in a bat of an eye," says daughter Opal Symanski.

"She could make divinity that was always perfect," daughter Linda Helgoth says. "Divinity depends on the right temperature, humidity, ingredients. ... She never had a batch of divinity fail."

"She never got tired of doing it. She never complained," daughter Dee Schreiter says.

The grown children around the table think back.

"She'd sing to us," Symanski says. "She'd sing, 'You Are my Sunshine,' 'Down in the Valley.' ... She'd sing the old songs. 'Que Sera, Sera.'"

FOR A LONG TIME the family thought there was nothing Harold couldn't do. In his later years, the family says, he could hardly do anything. Severe arthritis finally forced him from the farm in the 1970s.

"If Dad could have he would have farmed to the end," Symanski says. "He'd always be looking at ads for tractors."

Instead, the couple spent the bulk of their time with their children, twenty-five grandchildren, and ten great-grandchildren, playing games and teaching everyone to fish. Catherine traveled with some of her children, even taking a trip to Hawaii. Harold refused to leave the only state he ever knew.

As they grew older, the couple continued to nag each other when they were together and worry when they were apart.

"It kept them sharp," Jim Helgoth says. "They weren't outwardly affectionate. It was the way they grew up, I think."

As the last of Harold's lives ran out, Catherine visited him in the hospital. With the family gathered around him, he hadn't responded to anything all day.

"She came in and he opened his eyes," Symanski says. "He focused on her."

If You Squeeze a Moment, What Comes Out?

Aimee Joan Grunberger

FROM WHERE SHE SAT IN HER STUDY, she could see through the town.

She saw the pettiness and politics. She saw the people hurrying around and the squabbles.

"These people need cancer," Aimee Grunberger said.

She had recently read in the newspaper about the latest political infighting. Inside her body, a tumor coursed.

"These people need cancer," she had said. "Not enough to kill them, just enough to make them see what's important."

It was something she wouldn't wish on anyone. To a degree, it was something she would wish on everyone.

"It's not that there's too much cancer; it's just that it's badly distributed," Michael Holleran says, expanding on his wife's words.

"Some people get it all, and that's too much. We'd all be better off if we had just a little. It would be a tonic."

For Aimee Grunberger, it was a tonic she first tasted that day in the doctor's office:

It was March, I was 39.

After diagnosis, the doctor kept talking. There was something wrong with his mouth. I had never seen such a deep pit. I thought if I looked way down into that hole, I might get sucked in. His head was acting funny, too— it seemed to stretch to the ceiling and then get very wide, blocking out the X-rays backlit behind him. With his head distorting, his mouth black and moving, I was glad to catch a few clear words " ... need to act quickly."

I got up, got dressed and reentered the waiting room. The children were sitting there. They put down their tattered magazines and looked up at me. Their feet didn't quite reach the floor.

A mother, teacher, and volunteer, Grunberger still found time to live her life at full speed. A poet, she always found the time to choose her words carefully.

Aimee Joan Grunberger died March 27, 1998, in Boulder, of complications from breast cancer. She was forty-four.

LEE CHRISTOPHER REMEMBERS when her good friend told her the news. Christopher handed her a leather journal.

"(Aimee) said, 'What's it for?' and I said, 'It's because you need to start writing about this.' "

Grunberger's poetry had already appeared in prestigious journals, and she was a two-time finalist for the Walt Whitman Award of the Academy of American Poets. She earned master's degrees from Brown University and Boulder's Naropa Institute (now Naropa University), and taught at Naropa's summer writing program. In 1992, Boulder-based Dead Metaphor Press published a book of her poems, *Ten Degrees Cooler Inside*. "She was only forty-four, and she had a late start," says Jack Collom, a friend and former professor at Naropa. "There were many poems in which she employed a lot of sarcasm and mordant wit about herself or the world."

Some of her poetry drew on life experiences in Rhode Island, where she worked for a time as a therapist at the Providence Veterans Administration Hospital (now the Providence VA Medical Center), dealing mainly with Vietnam veterans suffering from post-traumatic stress.

After doctors diagnosed her with breast cancer, Grunberger turned again to words, scribbling thoughts on scraps of paper. Lines, turns of phrase, something she heard, something she saw, or felt.

"Going through her papers, something that was very personally evocative was to come across the scribbles that were the early germs of her poems, and often very different from the polished pieces I was familiar with," Holleran says. "It wasn't a full-blown poem that came to her; it was some image, some set of lines, something that might fit into a poem as she worked."

The scraps soon filled the notebook, as a sprawling poem on mortality and cancer called "The Language of Stones."

"*What would you have done with forty years?*" she wrote. "*What does anyone do?*"

"It's a triviality when we say it, but there is something to living every day as if it's your last, understanding the preciousness of the time we have left," Holleran says. "Clearly, anyone who has dealt with cancer has a real understanding of that that none of the rest of us have."

> *what people fret about seems insane*
> *if you squeeze a moment what comes out*
> *this isn't bravery but momentum*
> *calendars ruffling sheets tearing off*
> *hair in the sink and on the pillow*
> *don't ask what we're doing next summer*

AFTER GRUNBERGER'S DEATH, Christopher met with Collom, sifting through the words. With the help of Aimee's brother, James, the family eventually plans to publish a collection of her poems about cancer.

"I don't know that Aimee would like to say that poetry was therapy," Christopher says, "but a side effect was that it was on the page. I think a poet always feels better when you put something on the page."

During the last few weeks of Grunberger's life, she could speak only a few dozen words a day. She used many of them for poetry.

Days before she died, she sat in a wheelchair, and her friends began a poetry exercise where each person adds one line to a free-form poem.

As they traded phrases, the last line was left to Grunberger:

Nothing is ever done.

The Shortest Obituary on the Page

Jonathon Richardson

SECTION 37, BLOCK 7, LOT 22, grave 9.

The cemetery worker bends down and finds a cement number in the ground near a headstone, then stands up and begins to count.

"Six, seven, eight, nine," he says, pointing to the plots. "There it is."

The gravesite is virtually impossible to find without help. There is no headstone, no marker of any kind. A browning patch of sod is the only indication of a recent burial.

On one side of gravesite No. 9 is smooth, untouched lawn. On another side, a dead, brown bouquet on another unmarked grave. The man in the new gravesite spent the bulk of his life working in the reflection of some of the city's most powerful people, in a job where he had to look up to meet their eyes. He spent much of his spare time in the background, at night, listening.

Thousands of people knew his face. Few knew him.

When it was printed in the newspaper, his was the shortest obituary on the page:

Jonathan 'Johnny' Richardson of Denver, a shoe-shine worker, died August 13, 1999 in Denver. He was 74.

No services were held.

He was born June 24, 1925. His interest was listening to jazz.

There are no immediate survivors.

JONATHAN RICHARDSON'S ESTATE fits in a cardboard container the size of a shoe box, kept in a lawyer's office on 16th Street.

There are a few photos in a large frame, a few loose snapshots, and about two dozen letters. In two envelopes are $8 in bills and about $20 in change. In another envelope are a few sterling silver rings—one with a fake diamond in the middle.

The letters in the box are from a woman named Karen, along with several photos of her.

Inside a stiff plastic sleeve are grainy, crinkly black and white photos. A young boy. A beautiful young woman wearing a corsage. A young girl. None of those photos are labeled.

It was all found in an apartment building in downtown Denver, along with Richardson's body. He had already been dead a couple days, which is how long it took before someone decided to check on him.

All of Richardson's mail is forwarded to the lawyer's office, where it will be kept with his other things for a year, unless a member of the family is found. So far, just a cable bill, a phone bill, and a refund from the apartment building.

The public administrator, the man in charge of Johnny Richardson's shoe box estate, says he hasn't given up hope for someone to claim it. The holidays are coming up. Sometimes, he says, letters show up from family members during the holidays.

IF ANYONE ASKED—if they really seemed interested—Johnny Richardson would tell them he was a man in an honorable trade, and a dying one.

If anyone asked, really asked, he would hold up his shoe polish-stained hands and show them the intricacies of the craft. He would show them how to snap the towel, how to rub with the right touch, how to give a good spit shine.

He learned the trade when he was a child, when someone handed him one of the old shoe-shine box kits. He still had his job when they found his body.

From his chair inside the old Stapleton Airport, Richardson applied the craft to tens of thousands of soles. For nearly two decades, businessmen would leave their oxfords with him to pick up before heading around the world. Friends would come in just to say hello.

Richardson told a buddy he would just keep on working at the airport until either he or Stapleton fell apart. He never really thought he'd outlast the airport.

"He was a private type of guy, but he was very cool for his age," says Tommy Rhine, who hired Richardson at his downtown shoe repair shop after the airport shut down and Richardson said he couldn't deal with the long drive to the new airport.

In the back of Rhine's shoe shop hang a few of the rare photos of Jonathan Richardson.

"He was always well-dressed," Rhine says, "and he liked to party."

When they tore down Rhine's building and he moved the shop a couple miles east, Richardson found another familiar face near the historic Brown Palace downtown.

"I had seen him around Denver since the sixties," says Lalo Sigala, who hired Richardson to shine at his barber shop on Glenarm Place. "He was real quiet. I think that's one reason people liked him. He was from the old school. Respect."

Inside Lalo's, an old barber pole still twirls. Underneath it, in chipped black paint, it reads, "SHINE."

"He had a laugh," says stylist Terri Gomez, from behind her chair at Lalo's. "He laughed with feeling."

The black vinyl on the shoe-shine chair is cracked, its steel forever stained black with polish.

"Lalo wouldn't let us put flowers on the chair when he died," Gomez says.

"Well, that's because it would make me cry," Sigala says.

Once the stylist leaves, he looks at the empty shoe-shine seat.

"I couldn't put flowers there because I'd have to see them all day long," Sigala says. "He was my friend, too."

THE WOMAN THEY USED TO CALL "Red" is as close to family as anyone can find.

"Johnny was good people," she says. "Johnny was everyday people."

At her home in Brighton, Karen Meggett's hair isn't as bright as it once was, but the origin of the nickname still shines through. Her pictures are the ones that dominate Richardson's box. Her letters are the ones he saved.

They met during the early 1970s, at the Cloud 7 Lounge on Welton Street. Like most of the bars Richardson once frequented, Cloud 7 is now a parking lot.

"When he first started coming in, they called him Batman, because he was always alone," Meggett says. Eventually they stopped calling him Batman, but, in many ways, she says, he remained alone.

In the photo on her table, Richardson is wearing what he usually wore: a full suit and bowler hat. He stood about five-foot-nine-inches and always kept himself slim.

"He always looked good. He always matched," she says. "Before he came over he would call and ask what color clothes I was wearing so he could color coordinate. He had all his hats in boxes and all his suits lined up."

Meggett and Richardson began dating in the 1970s and remained friends when she broke off the romantic relationship in the '80s. Her children from a previous marriage remember him as part of their own family.

"He was with us on Christmas and Thanksgiving," Meggett says. "We spent last Thanksgiving together, at Country Buffet on Alameda."

One of her daughters, Loretta Younger, says she remembers Richardson for his stories, including his account of attending the civil rights march in Selma, and the wisdom that came with his lifelong job.

"One piece of advice he gave me was that when someone puts you down, you just smile at them, and that makes them wonder what you're thinking," she says. "You just smile at them and walk away. That's what Johnny taught me."

INSIDE TURK'S SUPPER CLUB, the Denver Jazz Orchestra is warming up to play, which means that many of Jonathan Richardson's friends see a hole in the crowd.

"He knew all the players. He knew all the records. He even knew the rhythm sections and most people don't know those guys—most people only know the main players," says Denver saxophone player Freddie Rodriguez. "He knew if a guy had soul or not. He was like a musician because he knew."

Rodriguez is one of the many jazz musicians who first met Richardson at El Chapultepec, where he was known to prowl the club, quietly tapping, snapping, and clapping. It was at the 'Pec and other clubs, friends say, where Richardson spoke the language of jazz as fluently as many who played it.

"You could tell he was an enthusiast the way he walked, talked, and carried himself," says Samuel Bivens, longtime leader of the Denver Jazz Orchestra. "He understood jazz as an enthusiast. He was well-known in jazz circles as a … thoroughbred jazz enthusiast."

With Bivens, the conversations went beyond the music.

"We were contemporaries. We were both born between '25 and '30, so we were looking at some of the same situations faced by black men our age," Bivens says. "We had visited a lot of the same places. We had seen how things were."

Richardson's experience, Bivens says, shone through in his appreciation.

"His presence, his applause, all the areas of respect and accolades due a musician, he paid that respect. That's something we don't do too often," he says.

"Jazz is made up of the ethereal things that many people just don't understand. … He understood.

"Yes," Bivens says. "I remember Jonathan."

OVER THE YEARS, RICHARDSON watched the town he knew crumble. The economy motels he called home—The Dover, the Kenmark, the Cosmopolitan—were paved over. They even tore down the airport.

"He was part of the old times," says Frederick Moon, a friend from the old Cloud 7 days and the former executive chef at the Cherry Creek Inn. Now sixty-six years old, Moon lives by himself in Denver.

"We're just old dinosaurs. People forget about us," Moon says. "But we did contribute."

Moon says he remembers his friend for his quiet wisdom and love of music, but says he hadn't seen him around much, lately. Like Meggett, he had given up the night life, while, even at seventy-four years old, Richardson couldn't give up the jazz.

Inside Moon's apartment, colorful stuffed animals and trinkets cover every inch. He looks at the pink giraffe, multicolored monkey, and giant teddy bear that share his seat, and says he's found another vice.

"Some people go to bars when they retire," he says. "Now, I go to thrift shops."

Moon has been a bachelor all his life. Like his friend John, he says, he's used to being alone.

"There I go talking about me again, but this isn't a story about me," he says, and then smiles.

"Maybe in a few years you'll pick me out of the newspaper. Maybe in a few years, but not yet."

INSIDE THE BAR THAT IS nearly as old as Johnny Richardson, one of the few places that hasn't changed, Jerry Krantz snuffs out a cigarette.

"Sure, the old man, I remember him," says the owner of El Chapultepec. "He was in here pert' near three or four times a week, standing in the front or the back, drinking his brandy and Coke.

"I brought his brother in here to play."

Krantz points to the wall, at a picture of Jerome Richardson, the famous saxophone player who Johnny Richardson often claimed as his brother.

In a search to find any of Richardson's family after his death, the Denver County Coroner's office called Jerome Richardson. The sax player said he never heard of Jonathan.

"He once said he had kids in California. He said his brother was Jerome," Meggett says. "Now I really believe that Johnny was alone."

As the coroner searched for family members, Richardson's body entered a rotation of unclaimed bodies, which are buried at reduced cost through many local mortuaries and cemeteries. Bodies cannot be cremated without family permission.

Richardson's was the twenty-eighth body this year to enter the rotation.

JONATHAN RICHARDSON WAS BURIED without ceremony October 5, 1999, in a cloth-covered, pressed-wood casket, at Mount Olivet in Wheat Ridge.

Section 37, block 7, lot 22, grave 9 is in the back of the cemetery, with a view of the mountains.

Meggett says she hasn't seen the gravesite. She doesn't want to go down there until she can find it.

Inside her home, she takes out a slip of paper scrawled with the wording for the headstone.

> *What we keep in memory is ours forever*
> *Jonathan "Johnny" Richardson*
> *Jun. 24, 1925 — Aug. 13, 1999*

Meggett files away the paper. It will be another couple months before the headstone is ready. She hopes to gather up a few musicians then and have a proper service.

"You know, he always was going to write a book about his life," Meggett says. "He said he'd have to change the names, but that he could write a book about all the stories of his life."

She picks up one of the old snapshots and stares at his face.

"He always said he was going to write that book."

Acknowledgments

IN REPORTING THE STORIES WITHIN THIS BOOK, I've been invited into homes on Colorado's eastern plains to share homemade ham sandwiches and fresh-picked heirloom tomatoes. I've sat at the piano of a respected teacher and felt middle C worn thin by hundreds of tiny fingers. I've stared at my notebook countless times as the stranger across the table worked through another good cry. This book wouldn't be possible, foremost, without that openness and trust of the families reflected in the preceding pages. I also need to thank the people whose stories aren't included—believe me, I've learned something from you all.

Before those lessons, however, there were plenty of others taught by people who first led me to the words, among them: Betty Sheeler, who fed me books and showed me stories all her life; Bobbie Craig, the first English teacher that mattered, and John Calderazzo, the last one; Garrett Ray and Fred Shook, whose classes helped me understand the scenes of life; Greg Todd, who first believed in writing about nobody; Joe Watt, who treated the obituary page like the front page; Gary Burns, Doug Greene, Dennis Britton, Glenn

Guzzo, John Temple, Deb Goeken, Tonia Twichell, Jim Trotter, and the others who hired or supported me; Carolyn Gilbert, Alana Baranick, Stephen Miller, Marilyn Johnson, and other members of the International Association of Obituarists, for spreading the word; Jack Jackson, for watching over the stories from thousands of miles away, making many of them better; Pat Riley, for showing me where to find the words; and my sisters Amy and Cassie, just for putting up with me.

Thanks to Jim Pruett, for "getting it" before I had to explain, to G. Brown for the rockin' connection, and Kathy Kaiser for dealing with the past tense. Also, to Kim Mooney and everyone at Hospice of Boulder County (and for that matter everyone who's worked at any hospice anywhere).

When I walk into a room and understand how to take the time to listen, I nod to my parents, whose patience and support throughout my life has always been within reach when I needed them most.

Without the constant support of my wife, Annick, and powerful hugs from my son, James, many of these stories may never have reached the page. We've laughed and cried over them together, explored cemeteries hand-in-hand, and—even more importantly—created a pretty amazing tale all our own.